WARRIOR
DOG

★ ★

By Will Chesney

with Joe Layden

Feiwel and Friends
New York

A Feiwel and Friends Book

An imprint of Macmillan Publishing Group, LLC
120 Broadway, New York, NY 10271

Our books may be purchased in bulk for promotional, educational, or business use. Please
contact your local bookseller or the Macmillan Corporate and Premium Sales Department
at (800) 221-7945 ext. 5442 or by email at MacmillanSpecialMarkets@macmillan.com.

Library of Congress Control Number: 9781250244901

ISBN 978-1-250-24490-1 (hardcover) / ISBN 978-1-250-24491-8 (ebook)

Book design by Mallory Grigg

Feiwel and Friends logo designed by Filomena Tuosto

First edition, 2020

10 9 8 7 6 5 4 3 2 1

mackids.com

For Cairo

INTRODUCTION

This may not be quite the story you are expecting. I might as well make that clear now.

I served thirteen years in the US Navy, including eleven as a member of the elite Sea, Air and Land (SEAL) teams. I participated in hundreds of operations as part of the global fight against terrorism.

I was on the ground in Pakistan in the spring of 2011, when the world's most wanted terrorist, Osama bin Laden, was finally brought to justice.

It's fair to say that I have seen some battles. But that is only part of the story here, and not the most important part. I had the privilege of serving alongside some of the bravest men you could hope to meet.

But I also had the honor of working with an unsung hero whose role in the modern military is hard to comprehend—unless you served with him or one of his fellow four-legged warriors.

I grew up with dogs, but I didn't understand how much canines were being used in the military until I became a SEAL and began to hear the stories. I remember walking into a training room once, early in my career, and hearing the following order:

"Raise your hand if your life has ever been saved by a dog."

Most of the men in the room lifted their arms. They did not laugh. They did not smile. This was serious business.

A dog can save your life? Absolutely. In my case, many times over. Both on and off the battlefield.

This is my story, but it is also the story of one of those military working dogs, or MWDs. To be precise, he was part of a highly trained subset of MWDs known as combat assault dogs. And he was the most famous combat assault dog ever, thanks to his participation in the raid on bin Laden's compound. He was a canine SEAL named Cairo, a seventy-pound Belgian Malinois who jumped out of planes, fast-roped out of helicopters, swam across streams, sniffed out roadside bombs, and disarmed bad guys.

Cairo did everything expected of his human counterparts. He did it with loyalty and courage. I would have taken a bullet for him, and he did, in fact, take one for me. This is his book as much as it is mine. Maybe more.

I first met Cairo in the summer of 2008. I'd been in the navy for six years, almost all of it as a SEAL. I was stationed in Virginia, satisfied with my work, and not really looking for any big changes. But then I was introduced to the canine program, and it caught my interest.

Fortunately, in those days, experience was not a requirement for becoming a dog handler. All I had to do was express an interest in the job, and suddenly there I was, attached to a magnificent Malinois! German shepherds, Dutch shepherds, and Labrador retrievers have also been used in the military. But the Malinois, which is basically a smaller, more agile version of the shepherd, is the ideal military dog.

Not everyone is a "dog person." And not every SEAL wants to babysit an animal both at home and when they are on deployment. (A deployment is a long trip overseas to perform a series of missions. Most deployments last a few months.) My fellow SEALs were all happy to have Cairo out in front of us when we approached an enemy compound in the middle of the night. And when not on the job, he was a playful, friendly dog. Just about everyone loved him.

But to take on the burden of being a dog's handler? That was left to someone who really wanted the job.

That was me. Cairo was my dog. And I was his "dad."

The relationship between a handler and a canine SEAL is profound and intimate. It goes well beyond friendship. The training is challenging and endless. It is designed to foster not just expertise but a deep and complex attachment.

Anyone who has ever shared his life with a dog understands the two-way nature of the relationship. A dog relies on his master for food and shelter. He responds with unconditional love and loyalty. Take that relationship and multiply it by a hundred, and then factor in the almost unimaginable bond that is forged when a dog risks his life for you.

Then you'll get an idea of what it was like for Cairo and me.

So, yes, in a very real sense, I *was* Cairo's dad, as close to him as a father is to a son.

He was three years old when I met him. He had already graduated from a class of potential military candidates. He was a dog with not only freakish athletic ability but a tireless work ethic.

In other words, he was a dog who might become a SEAL.

But there was something else about Cairo that made him special: a laid-back personality that in other dogs might be cause for dismissal. A military working dog must be a fighter. In many cases that trait is not easily paired with companionship.

Cairo was different. He had the ability to throw a switch. He was gentle with people of all ages. But when it was time to go to work, he would work. He had a ferocious drive to hunt, perform, and serve. He was fearless.

That isn't quite true, of course. Everyone who has walked into battle experiences fear, pain, and exhaustion. Dogs are animals, driven by instinct. They naturally withdraw from danger. They rest when they are weary. Just like humans. It shouldn't come as much of a surprise to learn that it's almost as rare for a dog to become an MWD as it is for a human to become a SEAL.

It isn't for everyone. Let's face it: Most people don't want to enlist in the navy. And most people in the navy don't want to endure the agony of SEAL training. Of those who do take the plunge, most soon discover they are in over their heads. In fact, only 20 percent of the men who enter the thirty-week SEAL training program known as Basic Underwater

Demolition/SEAL (BUD/S) complete the program. The rest are weeded out not through injury or failure but through the simple act of surrender.

They quit.

The whole point of BUD/S is to find the true warriors—men who will not quit under any circumstances.

The same idea applies to developing military working dogs. Physical skill is useless if a dog freezes at the sound of a rocket propelled grenade (RPG) exploding into a hillside, or if he is afraid to enter a dark and dangerous building.

It's not natural for dogs to do these sorts of things. It's not . . . *normal*. But some of them do. Cairo was one of them. Did he realize he was risking his life for me and my brothers? Probably not. But he knew that his work was dangerous; I don't doubt that for a second.

In the mountains of Afghanistan, on mission after mission, Cairo was a fighting machine. He was a military asset as valuable as a rifle or night vision goggles. But when it was time to go home and hang out with Dad, he could do that as well. We'd sit on the couch and watch movies together. He'd eat steak right next to me. He would sleep in my bed. He could be trusted with strangers and kids.

He was a nearly perfect dog.

This book is my tribute to Cairo. It's a story about the amazing work he did in support of the US military, as well as what he did for me personally. We trained together, fought together, and lived together. He was, in many ways, my closest friend. I lost him for a while when our careers went in different directions, and then got him back long enough to care for him when his health failed. In return, he cared for me when I needed him most.

There is a code of selflessness among SEALs. While the work we do is serious and important, we are not, individually, *special*. We are a team united in purpose, none of us more vital than the next. I am proud of my military service, and of my work as a Navy SEAL, but I know there are men who sacrificed more. I share this story to honor my fellow soldiers, including a dog named Cairo, who often seemed just as human as the rest of us.

This is for you, buddy.

CHAPTER 1

Five feet ten inches tall. One hundred seventy-five pounds.

That's the average size of a US Navy SEAL. Not exactly a superhero. The truth is, SEALs for the most part look like ordinary guys. Fit and strong, yes, but not in a larger-than-life way. It's what's inside that counts. You can't judge a book by its cover.

There is no "typical" SEAL. We come from all walks of life, and from all parts of the country. I knew guys who struggled to get through high school. I knew others who were straight-A college graduates. Most of us were in our late teens or early twenties when we entered the SEAL training program. Others were much older. What we all had in common was a desire to serve our country at the highest level.

SEALs are involved in some of the most difficult missions in the military. The training is brutal because it is designed to select the people who are best suited for this kind of work. And it's always been this way. Although modern-day SEALs can trace their roots back to the underwater demolition teams of World War II, the official SEAL program did not begin until the 1960s. Since that time, BUD/S has been very effective at ensuring that only the strongest candidates reach the finish line and become SEALs.

SEALs are expected to be more than just physically fit. They must be smart and creative. They need to understand teamwork and discipline. SEALs frequently encounter unexpected situations, often during combat. They learn to think quickly and respond accordingly. It's a job with high stakes, so it makes sense that the training program is designed to find the people best suited to this type of service.

What made me think I could be one of the 20 percent who survived BUD/S? I don't have a good answer for that. Thinking about it now, as a thirty-four-year-old veteran, it seems almost crazy. I enlisted in the navy, entered the SEAL program, and . . . well, I just kept putting one foot in front of the other. There was nothing special about my background. I was an ordinary kid from a small town in Texas. I wasn't very big (five feet nine, 170 pounds). I wasn't a brilliant student or a great athlete. But I wouldn't quit. I knew what I wanted, and what I wanted was to be a Navy SEAL!

I graduated from high school in the spring of 2002. By that time, I had already enlisted in the US Navy. I was a senior in high school on September 11, 2001. On that day, terrorists hijacked two planes and flew them into the Twin Towers in New York City; another plane was hijacked and flown into the Pentagon, in Washington, DC; a fourth hijacked plane crashed into a field in Pennsylvania. The attacks killed thousands of innocent civilians.

Like everyone else, I was saddened and angered by a horrific event that has come to be known simply as "9/11." I wanted to get out there and help find the people responsible for the attack. I wanted to help make sure that it never happened again. I enlisted in the navy, but my plan all along was to try to become a SEAL.

I want to be honest about that. There is nothing wrong with traditional military service. It's vital to the American way of life, and the freedoms we value. But I was a seventeen-year-old kid itching to leave Texas and do something special with my life.

For me, it was the SEALs or nothing.

The thing is, in order to become a SEAL, you start by enlisting in the navy. I did that several months before graduating from high school. Because I was only seventeen, I needed my parents' permission to enlist.

My mother had some reservations. She questioned whether I knew what I was getting myself into. After all, our country had just been attacked by terrorists and at that time no one had any idea how our military would respond. My mother was scared that her son might be going off to fight a war. She was scared I might be killed. My father, however, was excited and proud that I wanted to be a SEAL. And that's the way I presented it to my parents. Not, "I want to enlist in the navy," but rather, "I'm going to be a SEAL." Not because it sounded better, but because it was what I believed.

To get into BUD/S, I had to go through basic training, also known as boot camp. I also had to pass the SEAL physical screening test (PST) test. The PST is designed to separate the wannabes from the serious candidates. I had spent a big chunk of the summer after I graduated from high school trying to prepare appropriately. I did a lot of running and swimming. I went to the gym and lifted weights. I was in good shape. But in boot camp, we also spent a lot of time in the classroom, studying navy customs and culture. It was important stuff for anyone who would be spending the next four years serving in the "regular" navy. But I started to worry about getting out of shape and not being able to pass the PST.

Fortunately, the recruits who had expressed an interest in the SEAL program were allowed two days of physical training per week. It wasn't much, but it was better than nothing. The physical training was directed by a pair of men who represented my introduction to the world of Navy SEALs. One guy was in his early thirties and incredibly fit. The other guy was probably in his fifties and also in great shape. They pushed us hard in training, but they were also supportive. It seemed like they wanted us to believe that we could one day join their ranks.

The SEAL screening test is rigorous. It includes five exercises (or "evolutions," as I would come to know them in BUD/S), each of which must be completed in a certain time frame. The minimum standard is as follows:

» 500-yard swim (12 minutes, 30 seconds)
» 42 push-ups (2 minutes)

- » 50 sit-ups (2 minutes)
- » 8 pull-ups (no time limit)
- » 1.5-mile run (11 minutes)

The five exercises are completed consecutively, so it's more like one big test than a series of individual tests. There is minimal rest time between events. It should also be noted that the standards listed above are merely that: minimum qualifying standards. If you hit those numbers you are allowed to enter BUD/S, where you will almost certainly be among the very first to drop out. BUD/S is challenging enough for the fittest and strongest candidates. For those who enter the program having met only the minimum standards, the failure rate hovers around 97 percent. To increase the odds of success, the navy recommends achieving better scores on the PST.

I was confident that I would easily meet the minimum standards. I wasn't even worried about the 500-yard swim, which, believe it or not, is a common barrier for many aspiring SEALs.

A lot of people come to BUD/S with a strong background in swimming. Some were competitive swimmers in high school or college. Some played water polo. Others worked as lifeguards. But not everyone fits this profile, and even those who do are often shocked to discover that the "wet" portion of BUD/S is about much more than swimming. When it comes to water, it's about survival and strength, and overcoming the natural fear of drowning. A lot of candidates drop out of BUD/S during water training, even though they are good swimmers.

I loved the water, but I was not a competitive swimmer. My high school did not have a swimming team, and my family wasn't exactly the country club type. I didn't spend a lot of time swimming laps when I was growing up. But I liked water: rivers, lakes, the ocean. Didn't matter. I was a self-taught swimmer who never had any issues taking care of himself in a water environment. I knew that if I was out on a lake or an ocean bay somewhere and the boat capsized, I could get to shore. What more did I need to know?

A lot, as it turned out.

The swimming portion of the PST was conducted in a pool, but the distance covered had to be executed using a combination of the breaststroke and sidestroke. I had never been taught either of those strokes.

But I learned. I wasn't the fastest swimmer, and I didn't have the best form, but I worked hard. In the end, I was one of only a few guys from my boot camp class who qualified for BUD/S. It took me more than one attempt, but that's not unusual. A lot of people fail to meet the standard on one or more events and have to retake the entire PST. With the help of the SEAL trainers and a lot of practice, I passed on the second try.

I was so excited. I couldn't wait to get to BUD/S!

It wasn't until I got there that I understood why most people can't wait to leave.

CHAPTER 2

I arrived at Naval Base Coronado in March of 2003. Coronado is a sprawling complex in a resort community on San Diego Bay in Southern California. It is home to the Naval Special Warfare Training Center, where the six-month BUD/S course is held.

There are several BUD/S classes each year, with overlapping schedules. I entered SEAL training as part of BUD/S Class 246. There were 168 men in our class; of that number, only twenty-two would reach the finish line. And yet, several others from previous classes would graduate with us as part of Class 246.

BUD/S was simultaneously one of the best and worst

experiences of my life. I would guess this is a sentiment shared by every SEAL. I wouldn't trade it for anything. It was horrible and exhausting. Sometimes it was weirdly funny. The purpose of BUD/S is to determine not just who wants to be a SEAL but who is really equipped for the job. When I arrived in Coronado, I knew I was part of the first camp. I didn't know yet whether I'd be part of the second.

BUD/S is divided into three phases of training. First Phase is devoted to physical conditioning. Second phase is devoted to swimming and underwater diving and training. The third phase is known as land warfare. But before you even get to First Phase, you have to go through indoctrination training, also known as "Indoc."

The navy understands that boot camp doesn't really prepare a recruit for the physical and mental demands of BUD/S. Jumping right into First Phase would result in a success rate of somewhere around 0 percent, is my best guess. To improve the odds, students new to BUD/S enter a pre-indoctrination stage known as Physical Training, Rest and Recuperation (PTRR). Here the emphasis is on preparation and fitness, along with medical screening to ensure that candidates are up to the challenge of BUD/S. Candidates from previous classes who have been rolled back due to illness or injury all end up in PTRR, where they train and recuperate while awaiting assignment to another class. For these students, PTRR can be a long and frustrating experience.

When numbers are sufficient, an entire class moves on to Indoctrination. Although technically BUD/S is a three-stage training program, Indoc is much more than just a warm-up. Ask anyone who has been through it: Indoc is where BUD/S really begins. It's five weeks of intense physical training and conditioning, and mental strain. Indoc is designed not only to prepare the class for the rigors of BUD/S but to introduce the customs and traditions that are part of the entire experience. For twelve hours a day you swim, run, climb ropes, navigate obstacle courses, carry inflatable boats, and generally experience exhaustion on a level you couldn't imagine. You also spend time in classrooms, absorbing lessons on the SEAL philosophy. There is a heavy emphasis on ethical and honorable behavior.

You also get yelled at. A lot!

The job of a BUD/S instructor is not merely to train but to push students to the breaking point. I'd been through boot camp, so I knew what it was like to have a drill instructor scream at me. But that was amateur hour compared to BUD/S. I sometimes felt like the instructors just enjoyed yelling at us and watching us suffer. But they were performing a vital service. Their job is to train young men for one of the most demanding positions in the military. Part of that job is to weed out everyone who isn't up to the challenge.

I learned on the first day of Indoc that everyone messes up. You might as well just admit your mistakes and make no excuses. If you were ordered to do ten push-ups, an instructor would stand over you, counting. He would give you credit only for the push-ups that were done perfectly. And, of course, there was no such thing as "perfect." As you can imagine, we all did hundreds of push-ups each day.

Every inspection resulted in some type of punishment. Make the slightest mistake and you'd find yourself running to the surf for a quick dip in 60-degree water. The dunking was typically followed by a roll in the sand, until your entire body was covered with sticky, hard granules. This was known as a "sugar cookie." And trust me, it's not as much fun as it sounds.

It's interesting. You go to BUD/S worrying about whether you might drown, or how well you will hold up while running endless miles in the sand while wearing heavy boots. You worry about whether your fear of heights will prevent you from scaling a twenty-foot rope wall during the obstacle course. But in the end, it's the simple stuff that drives you crazy: the sleeplessness, the bone-chilling cold that comes with being wet all the time, and the skin rubbed raw by wet clothes and sugar cookies.

The purpose of Indoc is to exhaust and scare the pretenders before the real work began.

If I can't handle this, how am I going to survive the next six months?

It was a brutal but effective strategy. We lost thirty people from Class 246 before First Phase even began. That's nearly 20 percent who decided that being a SEAL wasn't such a great thing after all.

So, they rang the bell.

Oh yeah. The bell. There was no quiet or dignified exit from BUD/S. You could quit any time. Instructors even encouraged quitting!

All you had to do was ring the drop-on-request (DOR) bell. Just walk over to the bell, grab the long, thick braided rope that hung temptingly from its opening, and give it three quick tugs.

Clang! Clang! Clang!

Relief was immediate. So was shame. And, often, regret.

But why do so many people feel this way? Washing out of

BUD/S is hardly embarrassing. Eight out of ten students fail to complete the program. Then they move on to some other type of job in the navy. What's the big deal?

In your weaker moments (and there are many of them during BUD/S), this is what you tell yourself. It is the lie that seeps into your sleep-deprived brain and tempts you with the promise of rest and recovery. Then you hear the bell ringing out across the base, and you know what it means: Someone has quit. You instantly picture that person changing into dry clothes and eating a warm meal, and then collapsing into a comfortable bed. For just a moment, you want to run to the bell yourself and end the suffering.

I thought about it a few times. Everyone does. But no matter how badly I wanted to quit . . . the sound of the bell always signaled to me that I was one step closer to the finish line.

I will not quit. You'll have to kill me first!

There were a few times during BUD/S when I felt like I might be risking my life. One of those was in First Phase, during a training exercise called "drownproofing." It was a test designed to teach the candidate ways to prevent drowning under the worst conditions. In drownproofing, we entered the deep end of a pool with ankles tied together and hands bound behind our backs.

It was a simple and frightening exercise. It tested not only a student's stamina but his ability to remain calm under pressure. If you didn't panic, drownproofing was a manageable exercise. You took a deep breath and sunk to the bottom of the pool. Then you kicked off the bottom and surfaced, took another deep breath, and repeated the cycle.

Over and over.

And that was just the beginning.

After repeating the bobbing exercise twenty times, we had to float for five minutes, then swim to the shallow end of the pool, turn around without touching the bottom, and swim back to the deep end. Then we had to dive to the bottom and retrieve a face mask. How did we do this with our hands tied behind our backs? Well, by using our teeth, of course.

I didn't have a big problem with drownproofing. It was less about being a strong swimmer than remaining focused and relaxed in the water. But some guys panicked and quit. There have been serious injuries and even a few fatalities in BUD/S, but it is extremely rare. The young men are strong and fit, and the Navy goes to great lengths to ensure their safety. Medical personnel constantly monitor candidates for signs of illness or injury. Meals are huge and frequent to ensure that students have the necessary fuel.

BUD/S is not inhumane. It is not torture.

It just sometimes feels that way.

First Phase was a lot like Indoc, with an emphasis on physical training, only much more intense. There were endless push-ups, miles of running in heavy sand, hours of time spent in the frigid surf of the Pacific Ocean. We were divided into teams and had races while carrying two-hundred-pound inflatable rafts over our heads. (These were known as "elephant runs.")

We never stopped moving.

The very worst part of First Phase was also the worst part of BUD/S. It was called Hell Week. And for a good reason. Hell Week was awful! It was five straight days of the hardest evolutions. Back-to-back. We had already experienced most of these exercises. What made Hell Week so much harder is that we were given almost no rest. We were barely even allowed to sleep. That's not an exaggeration. During the entire week, we slept twice, and for only a couple of hours each time.

For me, the ideal strategy for surviving BUD/S, and especially during this week, was to think of it as a series of small challenges rather than one gigantic test. Just try to make it from one meal to the next.

I learned very quickly the value of taking a positive approach to Hell Week. If we were instructed to lie down in the surf and let the cool water roll up over our faces, I would close my eyes and go to my "happy place." I'd imagine I was somewhere warm and calming. Pretty soon the worst of it was over and it was time to move on to the next awful exercise.

I have no explanation as to why this worked for me. Everyone had their own way of coping with the pain. Look at photos of trainees during Hell Week, and you'll see a row of guys on their backs in the surf, arms locked, bodies rigid. Some of them will be bug-eyed with fear. Others have their faces contorted in pain.

And some will appear to be almost asleep, as if they are oddly at peace with their surroundings.

That was me. I was one of the lucky ones.

Most people who quit during Hell Week did so in the first two or three days. If you made it to Wednesday, it was presumed you had the ability to get through Hell Week. And if you could get through Hell Week, the odds of getting through BUD/S tilted in your favor. In the final forty-eight hours, the instructors were a bit less vicious. They became more likely to encourage.

The final evolution of the week was on Friday morning. They called it So Sorry Day, because it featured an obstacle course through mudflats and sewage and barbed wire. I had never smelled anything so terrible! In the afternoon, we made our way back to the base, soaking wet and caked with mud. We were exhausted. As we assembled on the beach, the instructors planted a flag in the sand. Then one of them shouted through a bullhorn, "Class 246, Hell Week is secured!"

At first there was stunned silence. A few guys looked like they might cry. There were weary hugs, and then shouts of "Hoo-yah!" rang across the beach. We stood up as the instructors walked through our group. They shook our hands and smiled. These men had spent the previous five days treating us like dirt. Now they embraced us as brothers. I had never felt so proud in my life.

Afterward, I took a shower and put on some dry clothes. The instructors ordered pizza for everyone—and by pizza, I mean an entire large pizza for each surviving candidate. I sat outside and shoveled pizza into my face. Then I called my father to give him the news.

"Hey, Dad," I said . . . and then for some reason a mischievous thought crossed my mind. And I paused.

"What's up, Will? How's it going?"

"I'm sorry, Dad. I wanted to let you know that I didn't make it. I just quit."

"No way," he said. And that was it. I laughed into the phone.

"Yeah, you got me, Dad. You're right. I'm okay. Hell Week just ended. I made it."

There was another pause. I could almost see my father smiling.

"Good job, boy."

Early that evening I fell into bed and lost consciousness almost immediately. For the next twelve hours I slept like the dead.

It was, and remains, the best night of sleep of my entire life.

CHAPTER 3

Second Phase of BUD/S was eight weeks of diving instruction and practice, conducted in pools, training tanks, and San Diego Bay. By this point, the odds were now in our favor. Including rollbacks from previous classes, Class 246 ended First Phase with fifty students. We'd lose a dozen more in Second Phase. But in comparison to First Phase, it felt like the sound of the DOR bell was as rare as a smile from one of the instructors.

Not that it was easy. BUD/S was never easy. Safety is a big concern during Second Phase, because dive training can be dangerous. For this reason, we spent the first week studying physics and physiology and the basics of diving. We were required to pass written tests before getting in the water.

And then we moved on to Pool Week, where we got our first taste of actual scuba diving. We learned how to become comfortable underwater, even in a crisis. I don't care how tough you are, or how adept you are at swimming. When outside forces cut off your air supply or water leaks into your equipment, the first response is to seek relief. The second is to panic.

Second Phase was packed with evolutions and training designed to test a student's ability to cope with what feels like a near-death experience. After all, a SEAL might face even worse challenges on a mission. A few students simply couldn't cope with it and ended up dropping out.

I just kept telling myself: *Stay calm . . . stay calm.*

That was the key to surviving dive training. We were tossed into various bodies of water and forced to flirt with the sensation of drowning. It was scary, but after a while you got used to it. And if you didn't, you were gone.

A lot of the drills and tests were designed to promote teamwork and trust. For example, we'd sit at the bottom of the pool in pairs, sharing one mouthpiece. This was known as "buddy breathing." The idea was that in the middle of a mission, you might experience a problem with your equipment. The only way to survive would be to share oxygen. The exercise encouraged both teamwork and courage.

Other tests were more physical, like treading water without using your hands while wearing a weighted belt and all your scuba gear. Sometimes an instructor would swim by in the middle of an exercise and rip off your mask or air hose just to see how you'd respond.

The proper response was to calmly replace the gear. In the real world, any number of outside forces—from rough surf to a capsized boat—can cause you to lose your equipment. It's crucial to remain calm under even the most difficult conditions.

The hardest part of Second Phase was a test known as pool comp. It measured our fitness, knowledge of basic diving techniques, and ability to stay calm under pressure. The pool comp test involved jumping into the water with full scuba gear and then sitting on the bottom while awaiting "orders." We were expected to work through a series of challenges: untying knots in hoses, fixing problems with our tanks, replacing masks that had been ripped off. And we weren't allowed to come to the surface until we were done.

As with most tests in BUD/S, we were given two chances to pass pool comp. I passed on the first attempt, which was a huge relief. Everyone knew that if you made it through pool comp, you'd make it through Second Phase.

Near the end of Second Phase, we did get to make one really cool dive, a two-hundred-foot descent to a sunken ship that felt like the sort of scuba diving I'd always heard about. It was all part of the process. The navy didn't want us out in the ocean until we had demonstrated skill in a controlled environment.

By the time Second Phase ended, there were roughly forty members of Class 246 remaining. We were nine weeks away from becoming SEALs. The finish line was in sight. Finally, it began to seem real.

The navy handbook description of Third Phase is a mouthful of words about basic weaponry, tactical training, and demolition. But SEALs just call it "Land Warfare." Like everything else about BUD/S, it was exhausting and challenging.

It was also a lot of fun.

If you were to ask a civilian to describe what they thought SEAL training was like, they would probably come up with something like Third Phase. The training focuses on things like marksmanship and rock climbing, as well as explosives and navigation; Third Phase provides candidates with a chance to apply their skills and training. It simulates the conditions of a mission.

The pain and stress of physical training was combined with interesting and challenging field exercises. I'd be lying if I didn't admit that it was cool to blow things up or to use a variety of weapons. You don't become a SEAL if you don't like guns and explosives. It's part of the job.

For the last five weeks of Third Phase, we moved offshore to an island training facility. This was the site of the notorious 5.5-mile swim.

It's hard to describe just how hard it is to swim 5.5 miles. In the ocean. In rough 60-degree water. And did I mention the sharks? Okay, I'll say it now. There are sharks all around this island. Big, nasty, man-eating sharks, including the granddaddy of all ocean carnivores: the great white shark.

Now, the truth is, in all the years that the navy has conducted BUD/S training, there has never been a single case of a shark attack on a trainee. But when you step into the water for the 5.5-mile swim, knowing you're going to be out there for more than four hours, wearing a slick black wetsuit and fins that might confuse any hungry shark into thinking he's looking at a seal, rather than a SEAL, it does make you wonder. As most people know, the seal is at the top of the great white's menu. This island is home to a large seal colony. Where there are seals, there are sharks, and there were lots of seals nearby.

The possibility that one of us might get eaten was a source of humor among the instructors. They took great delight in letting us know that we'd probably have company during the ocean swim. We were told that shark encounters were not just possible but likely. If we ran into one of the toothy monsters, we were supposed to hold our ground and fight back.

Sure.

For safety reasons, each of us was assigned a partner ("swim buddy") for the test.

At one point a seal began swimming alongside me and my swim buddy, Connor. And not just for a couple of strokes. He was with us for maybe a half mile or more. You don't realize how big seals are until one is swimming next to you, nor do you realize how beautiful and graceful they are. They really do look a bit like dogs. If you get close to one in the water, they have similar personalities, too. We even played around with him like he was a puppy. It occurred to me only later that we might as well have been swimming with shark bait!

I had been worried about the ocean swim since the start of BUD/S. But it turned out to be not that bad. I mean, it was long and boring and painful, but at some point, it became apparent that we were going to reach the finish line. I was filled with a sense of pride and accomplishment. This was the last serious obstacle standing between me and graduation from BUD/S, and now it was nearly over.

But as we broke the surf line and slogged up the beach, we were hit with a surprise. We had failed to complete the swim before the mandatory cutoff time.

"Get some rest, gentlemen," one of the instructors said. "You'll be doing this again tomorrow."

This was perhaps the worst thing I had ever heard in my life. We were completely exhausted. Instead of being allowed to celebrate, we were told that we would have to repeat the torture in less than twenty-four hours. I was angry and confused. I didn't even know there was a cutoff time for the ocean swim. Maybe I should have paid closer attention.

I ate a big meal that evening and passed out as soon as I hit the bed. I woke to the stark realization that today would be even worse than yesterday. I was so sore I could barely walk. Despite a solid eight hours of sleep, I was foggy and exhausted. The idea that we were going to get back in the water and swim 5.5 miles all over again seemed crazy. They might as well have asked us to swim to Hawaii. For one of the few times during my entire BUD/S experience, I felt a sliver of doubt.

This can't be happening . . .

But it was. While the rest of the class slept in, Connor and I, along with a half-dozen other failures, dragged ourselves out of bed and began to dress. In the fresh light of the morning, we were instructed to prepare all our gear for the ocean swim. We went through the pre-swim inspection, just as we had the day before. We were yelled at and told we were useless. We were threatened with expulsion if we didn't perform better on this day.

We went to the beach and limped into the water. Only a few times during BUD/S did I feel defeated before an evolution even began. This was one of those times. While I was standing in the water, a wave crashed over me, causing me to lose one of my swim fins. Without the fins, the 5.5-mile swim would have been almost impossible. With only one fin . . . well, I can't even imagine the result.

I looked at Connor. He shook his head.

"We got this," I said, trying to sound encouraging. I don't think it worked.

And then, just as we were about to begin swimming, a miracle happened.

"Okay, everybody out!" an instructor yelled. "Today's your lucky day. We're going to give you credit for yesterday's swim."

Wait . . . what?

I looked at Connor. We both smiled. And then we laughed. Turns out they were just messing with us. If I wasn't so tired, I might have said something. But I was just happy it was over. In a matter of seconds, the worst day of BUD/S had become the best of days. I even caught a lucky break: Someone found my missing swim fin and handed it to me as we walked out of the water, so I didn't get chewed out for losing my equipment.

A few minutes later, we joined the rest of our classmates for the ceremonial raising of the flag, which we did every morning while reciting the Pledge of Allegiance. With the sun on my face, and the ocean swim behind me, I spoke the words aloud. They had never sounded so sweet.

Graduation was held on November 21, 2003, on a clear morning in Coronado. We all wore crisply pressed dress blue uniforms with white caps and spit-shined shoes.

I'd always been a fairly easygoing guy, not real emotional. These traits helped me get through the roller-coaster ride of BUD/S. But I'd be lying if I said that graduation wasn't a powerful day.

Although rollbacks from previous classes left Class 246 with roughly forty graduates, only twenty-two of the original 168 remained. You could see the pride on everyone's faces, and the joy of being reunited with friends and family. My parents both attended graduation, which was nice. They didn't get out of Texas very often, so this was a treat for them. It gave me a real sense of satisfaction and pride to walk up and receive my certificate, and to see their smiling faces.

The hated DOR bell in this setting was transformed into a symbol of teamwork and triumph. At the end of the graduation ceremony, three different students all were asked to ring the bell exactly once. As the final bell sounded, we threw our hats into the air and shouted.

"Hoo-yah!"

BUD/S was just the first step in the long journey to becoming a SEAL. There would be many more months of training and testing. Along the way I'd receive the Special Warfare insignia, also known as the SEAL Trident, that signifies membership in the SEAL brotherhood. While we might all have felt like SEALs that day in Coronado, and rightly proud of having survived BUD/S, there was so much more to learn.

A Navy SEAL is years in the making.

CHAPTER 4

What most people do not realize is that SEALs spend a lot more time training than they do on missions. There are years of training before the first time a SEAL embarks on a mission, and months of training between deployments. It never ends. Sometimes the training is pretty much what you expect it to be: hiking and camping in the wilderness, or jumping out of airplanes.

But sometimes there are opportunities that you never imagined. If you keep your mind open, they can change your life.

By 2006, I was a member of SEAL Team 4, stationed in Virginia. I loved everything about the job. It was my entire life. As laid-back as I might have been while growing up, I was driven and focused when it came to my career as a SEAL. I knew that one day I wanted to move up and be part of the most elite SEAL team.

Just being part of the SEALs was great, but everyone knew that the elite team was the best of the best. It drew the most challenging missions around the globe.

Not every SEAL dreams of making it to the elite team. But many do, and I was certainly one of them. I knew it would be a long journey, but I did everything I could to make myself a strong candidate. I went to the right training schools. I got certified in multiple areas. And I did the best job I could while I was on SEAL Team 4. The most critical factor in being selected to screen for the elite team was a recommendation from your current team leaders. I knew I had to have a stellar reputation.

I knew what my future would look like.

Or at least I thought I did.

In 2006, while on a training exercise in the mountains of Kentucky, I was exposed to a relatively new program within Naval Special Warfare. The SEALs had recently begun using military working dogs, and they wanted to give us a sneak preview.

I had a vague notion that dogs were used in law enforcement and some aspects of the military, but I knew almost nothing about military working dogs, and even less about how they might be employed in the SEALs.

What I saw on this day was a real eye-opener.

It was a short demonstration, just two men and a dog. But what a dog it was! The handler explained that the dog was a Belgian Malinois. I'd never even heard of the breed. It looked like a German shepherd, only slightly smaller and leaner.

"Let me tell you a little bit about this guy and what he can do," the handler said.

There were about sixty of us in attendance. We all stood around, sort of marveling at the dog's physical strength and beauty, but unsure what to expect. I'm not saying we were skeptical or negative in any way. We were just curious. In my time as a SEAL, I was open to the idea of using any tool that could make my job easier and safer. I think most guys felt that way.

The handler told us all about the Malinois's incredible sense of smell, how he could detect an explosive odor better than any man-made technology currently. Obviously, there were any number of ways in which this skill could be utilized: sniffing out roadside bombs in Iraq before they had a chance to kill a Humvee full of American soldiers; detecting an improvised explosive device (IED) that might be hidden near the perimeter of a compound in the mountains of Afghanistan. The dog's ability to track scents could also be used to find bad guys hiding in a building.

There were actually two handlers. One of them put on a bite suit and began walking. The suit was a heavily padded outfit that covered his torso and extremities but made it very hard to move. The handler wobbled awkwardly from side to side as he moved away.

Meanwhile, the other handler kept a firm grip on the harness of the Malinois. The dog clearly knew what was happening. He did not strain or pull against the handler's grip, but his body was tight, his eyes fixed on the target moving slowly away from him. I noticed the Malinois shifting his weight, bouncing lightly on his paws. Like a racehorse in the starting gate, he was eager to run.

The man in the bite suit kept walking across an open field until he was perhaps fifty meters away. He stopped and turned to face the other handler and the dog. Then he waved his hands and began running. Well, shuffling, really, but still, he had a big head start. I wondered how long it would take the dog to run him down, and what would happen when he reached the target.

The answers to both questions came soon enough. The handler released the dog and shouted a word I did not recognize. Instantly, as if shot from a gun, the Malinois burst into a dead sprint. An audible gasp went up from the crowd, the sound of appreciation and wonder. I had some athletic dogs when I was a kid, but I had never seen anything like this. The Malinois, seventy-five pounds of muscle, looked more like a greyhound, skimming across the ground so effortlessly that he seemed almost to be flying. In a matter of seconds, he closed the gap and finished with an explosive pounce.

As the man in the bite suit fell to the ground, the dog attached himself with his teeth. I had never seen such fierceness in a dog. And I had owned pit bulls and rottweilers! There were more gasps from the crowd, followed by laughter, and then some shouts of approval and respect. It was like watching one of those nature videos where a cheetah runs down a gazelle or a shark launches itself into a sea lion.

The dog was less than half the size of the man, but completely in control of the situation. As the guy writhed on the ground, yelping and flailing his arms in a futile attempt to discourage his attacker, the other handler jogged across the field. He had a big smile on his face as he put a firm hand on the dog's harness and issued another command. The Malinois loosened his grip, and the handler pulled him off the target.

And that was about it. The handler in charge of the demonstration thanked us for our time. He told us that soon enough we'd find ourselves on deployment with military working dogs. I suppose it's possible that a few guys simply didn't see the value of bringing a dog out on a mission. I saw the Malinois for what it was: a tool. And an impressive one at that.

Still, I never imagined that the canine program would have much of an impact on me personally. At the time I was focused on being a SEAL team "operator." A fighter. There wasn't room in my head to think about all the ways a dog might one day work itself into my life. That would happen much later.

CHAPTER 5

No one quits the training team.

Well, that's not quite true. I'm sure it happens occasionally. But for the most part, a SEAL who is offered a chance to screen for the elite team will not withdraw by choice. He is part of a training unit known as "training team." Survive this six-month program, and you're promoted to the most elite SEAL team.

In BUD/S, the vast majority of trainees simply aren't up to the challenge, and they know it. They either don't want it bad enough, or they can't fight through the pain. Either way, the outcome is the same: They quit.

The training team is different. The training is focused as

much on performance as misery. It's all geared toward developing skills that will be used on missions. The goal is not to force people to quit, but rather to select the best candidates for the job. This is done through combat and survival training as well as through psychological testing. More than half of the people who start the training team are eventually asked to leave.

I started in the fall of 2007, after two deployments to Iraq. Most of the training took place in Virginia. The hardest thing about it was knowing that I couldn't simply "will" myself to the finish line. I had to achieve required scores and times on a variety of tests. I had to prove I was an appropriate psychological fit for the elite team. In the end, it wasn't up to me. All I could do was work hard, try to maintain a good attitude, and hope I wouldn't be asked to leave.

I never was.

At the end of six months I graduated and became one of the youngest guys on the elite team. Graduates are assigned to one of four squadrons, each with approximately fifty members. I was lucky. I got assigned to a squadron where I already knew a few guys, which made the transition a little easier.

Training provided endless opportunities for the new guys to find their niche, and then they would concentrate on that specialty. Some guys liked skydiving, for example. Other guys liked sniper training or climbing.

I liked dogs.

I mean, I liked a lot of the other stuff, too, but I found myself drawn to the dogs, probably more out of curiosity than anything else.

The history of working dogs within the Navy SEALs can be traced back as far as the Vietnam War, although they weren't widely used until after the events of 9/11. The conflicts in Iraq and Afghanistan frequently involved hidden explosive devices. There, it became apparent that specially trained dogs, with their extraordinary sense of smell and ferocious prey drive, could be a huge asset. As a result, demand for the dogs increased, leading to an expansion of programs designed to train both military dogs and handlers.

Rather than simply acquire dogs from other sources, the SEALs began training their own dogs, much as the army had been doing for years. A small program in Virginia had been in place for a couple of years by the time I came along. This program was specifically designed to provide military working dogs for the SEALs.

In order to be integrated into the ranks, the dogs had to become comfortable with their human counterparts. And we had to be comfortable around them. As one of the new guys, I was a bigger part of this desensitization process than some of my more experienced teammates.

It was all pretty basic stuff. We'd watch the handlers work with the dogs, then take a turn at moving them around, very gently just guiding them through spaces. The dog would be passed from soldier to soldier. Sometimes while we were doing shooting drills, the dogs would walk around us or weave through our legs. The idea was to simulate the conditions of battle so that they would be comfortable around gunfire and explosions and respond positively to anyone in the unit.

I wouldn't say I had any intention of making a career out of being a dog handler. But I liked the look and temperament of the dogs, and I was curious about how they would perform on a mission.

The answer came during my next deployment, in the spring and early summer of 2008. We were based in Kandahar Province, in Afghanistan. The missions in Afghanistan were different from what I had experienced on previous deployments. In Iraq, most of the fighting took place in cities. In

Afghanistan, our missions took us out into rural and mountainous regions, or to small villages, on an almost nightly basis.

We had two dogs embedded with us on that deployment. Their names were Falco and Balto. Night after night, I watched them do amazing work. There were virtually no restrictions on where we could take them. If we had to jump out of a helicopter while hovering fifty or a hundred feet above ground, the handler would hook the dog into his line and fast rope with him. If we had to parachute in (which wasn't common, but did happen), the dog would be placed in a harness and a large pouch, attached to his handler, and the two of them would jump together. It was awesome to witness this, especially because the dogs always seemed so calm.

Although they didn't carry weapons, Balto and Falco, both Belgian Malinois, were outfitted with nearly as much high-tech equipment as the rest of us.

And they deserved every ounce of it!

You had to see the dogs on a nightly basis to truly appreciate their contributions. It wasn't just that Balto and Falco could sniff out explosive devices or run down an enemy fighter before he had time to hurt one of our team. They could also be sent into a building, where their movement could be tracked with cameras. This made it possible for us to have a better idea of what we would see once inside. Not only would the dogs provide us with a clear picture of a structure but they would also frequently find insurgents and either attack them or hold them at bay until we arrived.

(An "insurgent" is what the enemy was often called in Afghanistan. It means someone who is part of a rebellion, but not necessarily part of a country's official military force. The enemy in Afghanistan and Iraq were terrorists . . . rebels . . . insurgents. It was complicated, so we often just referred to them as "bad guys.")

At first, I barely noticed the dogs. They were just sort of there, behaving appropriately. Then I started to pay closer attention, and I'd see the little things they would do and how fiercely loyal and reliable they were. It was common to come back from a mission and talk about what had gone down. Invariably, someone would bring up one of the dogs.

"You see what Balto did out there, man?"

"No, I was on the other side of the compound. What happened?"

"Practically took someone's arm off. Guy never had a chance."

Sometimes the stories were quite dramatic. There was one

time, for example, when a group of our men were walking through a field in a line. The dog was on the left end of the line, off lead, and actively following a scent. He was excited, which is usually a sign that a dog is onto something.

This type of situation is ripe for the possibility of an ambush, so the dog's handler gave a command and let him go. The dog ran down the line of men at full speed, from the far left to the far right, near a tree line. He stopped suddenly and tore into the ground in front of him. A human cry went out, loud and piercing. There was a flutter of grass and leaves and other debris as an insurgent popped up.

This particular bad guy had an AK-47 automatic rifle in his hands. The dog was attached to his leg.

They weren't more than a few meters from our unit.

I was a good distance away from the encounter, so I didn't see the way it ended. But a lot of guys wanted to talk about it afterward. As the dog ripped into his leg, the insurgent hesitated just long enough to present a close and easy target for our unit. He was shot and killed at close range, and the mission went on without any casualties on our side. If not for the dog's help, that ambush would have ended differently. Some of our guys would have been killed.

As the deployment went on, I would come to realize that

a dog saving someone's life wasn't a rare occurrence. It happened all the time. When you're going out on operations practically every night, over the course of a four-month deployment, the close calls begin to add up.

After a while, I began to think of Balto and Falco as members of the squadron. I began to think of them as part of our family.

These dogs were fighting-and-tracking machines. They also could be really cute. Balto's handler even taught him how to open doors! Which was quite a trick, but also freaked people out.

Some dogs were more affectionate than others. Like humans, each had their own personality. In general, they could be trusted to hang out with us when we got back from a mission. They were tools, yes. They were weapons. But they also were . . . *dogs*. If you were a dog guy, like me, you felt affectionate toward them. And the fact that they were such loyal and reliable soldiers strengthened the relationship.

We were halfway through that deployment when I decided that I wanted to be a dog handler. This was not a decision to be made lightly. While dogs were extremely important to our work, the job was quite different from what I had done in the past.

Not everyone wanted to be a dog handler. First of all, you had to really like dogs. Second, you had to accept that the job was a supportive position. Unlike other members of the team, a dog handler was expected to manage and care for his dog at all times, while also serving as an operator. It was a complicated job. Once a handler released his dog, he became another soldier, armed and ready to fight. But he had to balance those two priorities: fighting and taking care of his dog. The dog handler was rarely the first guy in a room. Much of the time he was outside, on the perimeter, looking for explosives or holding security. This job was no less important than any other job on a mission.

But it was . . . *different.*

Not only that, but the responsibility of being a dog handler never seemed to end. Operators would return from a mission, take care of their gear, and then hang out and relax. The dog handler . . . well, he had to take care of the dog. 24/7. Some guys, like Frank, loved it. Frank was Falco's handler. He was a Master at Arms (a Master at Arms is like a law enforcement officer in the navy). He wasn't a SEAL. But he knew his stuff when it came to dogs, and he could handle himself in a firefight. I was intrigued by the challenge of balancing these dual responsibilities.

As the deployment wore on, I spent a lot of time with both dogs, but especially with Falco. I really liked his personality. I also knew that Frank was planning to give up his role as Falco's primary handler, which meant Falco would need a new partner. Frank liked the idea of my assuming responsibility for Falco because he wanted to know that his dog would be in good hands. The rest of the guys were only too happy to let me apply for the job because . . . well, somebody had to do it, and this way it wouldn't be one of them.

One night late in the deployment, we went out on a mission. As often happened, we divided into two assault teams. Each team was supposed to track a specific target. I was not on Frank's team that night, so I didn't see exactly what happened, but I heard the story afterward. Apparently, Falco caught someone hiding in a ditch, lying in wait and preparing for an ambush. As he was trained to do, Falco jumped on the guy. Unfortunately, he wasn't alone. This was the most dangerous situation for a dog: coming upon more than one person. As Falco held on to the first guy, just as he was trained, the second guy shot Falco several times.

The rest of the team quickly responded and shot both

enemy soldiers, but not before Falco was critically wounded. By the time I arrived and saw him being loaded onto a helicopter, he was already dead. The loss hit me hard, but not nearly as hard as it hit Frank. He was devastated, almost as if he had lost a family member or a fellow soldier.

Which, in a way, he had.

We held a memorial service for Falco back on the base. Frank got up and said a few words. There were tears and salutes. Afterward, we did what we would have done for any of our brothers: We talked about what a great soldier and friend Falco had been to all of us. We told stories. We shared a cake in his honor. We celebrated his life and service. We laughed more than we cried.

We said goodbye.

Falco was cremated. His ashes were placed in an empty ammo can and presented to Frank. They went home together.

CHAPTER 6

Most dogs that work in law enforcement and the military are not bred in the United States. Instead, they are products of European sport programs, like *Schutzhund* in Germany or KNPV in the Netherlands. They have received certificates acknowledging their ability to track, bite, detect scents, and follow commands.

These dogs are not ready for military missions the moment they are acquired, but they do possess the basic skills and training to be successful. In most cases, the dogs are two to three years old by the time they are purchased by American clients. In many ways, they are the same age as their human counterparts in the military: late adolescence or early adulthood.

They are strong, fit, and ready to be molded into a unique asset.

The dogs aren't cheap. A Malinois puppy with solid bloodlines might cost as much as two thousand euros ($2,300). But his value can easily quadruple by the time he is sold to a buyer in the US.

Several months before I was introduced to Cairo, he was acquired during a European buy trip organized by a company called Adlerhorst International. Adlerhorst is a Southern California business serving police K-9 units and the military as well as private clients. The buyers spent more than two weeks visiting dog clubs in different countries.

They found Cairo on the very first day, when they visited a club in the Netherlands in the village of Best. Most of the dogs were either German shepherds or Belgian Malinois, with a handful of Dutch shepherds sprinkled in. The buyers included a trainer named Don Christie, who was a representative from the SEALs. He watched with the others as the canine candidates were put through their paces in scent detection and tracking. All the dogs tested well. A few were exceptional, especially when it came to the "bite test." In that test, one of the handlers put on a bite suit and encouraged the dogs to attack. Of the dozen or so dogs assessed at the club, Cairo was the most determined biter. That made him one of the most promising military candidates.

Cairo was sturdily built, roughly seventy pounds of muscle, with good teeth, ears that did not flop over, and a thick, healthy coat. His coloring was darker than a typical Malinois: deep brown, with flecks of black throughout the legs and torso, giving way to a darker hue along the head and snout. His big brown eyes were bright and alert, signaling an eagerness to work.

"He looked great," Don Christie recalled. "And he was very strong. I remember him biting calmly on the suit, and just hanging on. In a bite test, you yell at the dog. You try to dissuade him. Cairo was not easily dissuaded."

The group selected a couple of dogs from that particular club. Cairo was one of them. He was placed in a traveling kennel and joined the buyers in their utility van. Then it was on to the next club, and the next town . . . and the next town and the next club after that. By the end of the trip, Adlerhorst had acquired more than thirty dogs. Don Christie was given his pick of the litter. He selected eight dogs, including Cairo. Those dogs were shipped to Virginia to begin training as military working dogs.

Most of the dogs in this class were Belgian Malinois. A few were Dutch shepherds. There were no German shepherds. All three of these breeds are smart and energetic, but the Malinois is the most compact and athletic. That explains its popularity with law enforcement agencies and the military. Like the German shepherd, the Malinois is physically impressive. His appearance can be discouraging to criminals . . . and reassuring to law-abiding citizens.

Both the German shepherd and Malinois have an extraordinary ability to detect certain scents. All dogs have a sense of smell far greater than humans can imagine. But even among dogs, both the German shepherd and Belgian Malinois are unique. According to the American Kennel Club, the Malinois is ranked No. 6 among all breeds in scent ability; the German shepherd is No. 4, surpassed only by a trio of hunting and tracking dogs: the beagle, basset hound, and bloodhound.

It probably goes without saying that you wouldn't want to take a beagle into combat, let alone a slow-footed basset hound. Military working dogs have to be good at scent detection. But they also need speed, strength, and agility. For a long time, the German shepherd was the most popular breed for work in law enforcement and the military. But today the

Malinois is preferred. While the Malinois has nothing on the German shepherd when it comes to brainpower or strength, it does have other advantages. The Belgian Malinois is built for military work. It is quicker and more stable. It is better at handling uneven terrain. It is slightly smaller than the shepherd, so it is more easily transported. It also seems to be less prone to illness and injury.

The Belgian Malinois and German shepherd are both great dogs. But the Malinois is simply better suited to military work.

Once they arrived in Virginia, all eight dogs were immediately put through a series of tests by Christie and his training partner, Jim Hagerty, a former dog handler with the Los Angeles Police Department. The trainers ran the dogs through exercises and obstacle courses. They exposed the dogs to gunfire and other explosions. Most "regular" dogs hate loud noises. Through breeding and training, MWDs are less sensitive. But a single clap of thunder or lightning strike is not the same as a firefight. These SEAL dogs would have to be calm under conditions that should, by all reason, cause them to panic.

Even a dog that is great at scent detection, tracking, and biting is virtually useless if he cowers at the first crack of gunfire. So you might as well figure out the dog's mental state right away. All eight of the dogs in this class passed the initial screening process (all but one would end up serving with the SEALs). And as the testing and training progressed over the course of the next six to eight weeks, a few stood out.

One of those standouts was Cairo.

He remained calm around gunfire and explosions. He scampered up multiple flights of stairs without hesitation. This might sound like a small thing, but in fact it can be a problem for even the sturdiest working dogs. They are instinctively distrusting of open staircases, which seem mysterious and dangerous. Some dogs refuse to climb stairs. Some freeze when they are halfway to the top. Some make it to the top and refuse to come back down.

None of those reactions is acceptable in the middle of a SEAL mission.

Cairo, for whatever reason, did not mind ascending or descending stairs. Even if they were open in the back and revealed a long and spooky drop to the ground, he was unfazed.

Cairo also had a personality that endeared him to his trainers. He was friendly, but not boisterous.

"He was a sweetheart," Christie recalled. "A very special dog—a fine example of what these dogs are bred to be. He was strong and enthusiastic. He was just . . . happy."

CHAPTER 7

Cairo was not my first choice. I might as well be honest about that.

We met in the summer of 2008. I'd gotten back from deployment and taken some time off for vacation. Now I was preparing to move on to my new role as a dog handler.

Of course, this did not relieve me of my other training commitments within the squadron. It was an additional responsibility. Which was fine. If longer days were the price to pay for being a dog handler, I was more than willing to make the investment.

Twelve-hour days didn't bother me in the least. I loved everything about being a SEAL: the training, traveling, missions, and friendships. I was keenly aware that I had beaten long odds. I was a kid from Nowhere, Texas. I had no military lineage, no great academic or athletic accomplishments. And yet I was part of one of the most elite military units in the world. I'd gotten to that level by working hard and refusing to quit. I wanted to do whatever I could to help the team.

Being a dog handler was a chance to do something different. It might not have been the most high-profile job, but after watching Falco and Balto in Afghanistan, I knew how important it was. I also thought it was a really cool assignment. I liked dogs. I was fascinated by their expanding role within the SEALs, and I wanted to be part of that expansion. Before I even showed up to the first dog training session in Virginia, I was excited about the opportunity to be a handler. And once I met the dogs, I was all in!

The introduction came during a half-day exercise at a training site not far from our base. The trainers had been working with this crop of eight dogs for two months, preparing them to be part of a SEAL team. Each dog would be assigned either to an operator or a Master at Arms. I knew ahead of time that, as a SEAL, I'd get one of my top choices. But they all looked great! I mean, I didn't know anything about military working dogs at that time, but every one of these guys looked like a thoroughbred.

Having already served with Falco and Balto, I felt comfortable around the dogs. But we were all reminded that while they were attractive animals, these were still attack dogs. They were also young and unaccustomed to the military life.

"I wouldn't try to pat them on the head or anything," one of the trainers said. "Think of them as weapons, not pets. Treat them with respect."

I thought that was kind of funny, but it was certainly a warning that had merit. The Belgian Malinois and Dutch shepherds introduced to us that day were gorgeous. Beneath the beauty, though, beat the hearts of warriors. Every one of these dogs was a ferocious fighter with an extraordinary prey drive. While they responded best to positive reinforcement, they also required a firm hand.

You had to show them who was boss, and you didn't do this by scratching them behind the ears and cooing at them like you might to a baby. Not in the beginning, anyway.

For much of the afternoon we were spectators, watching as the dogs ran impressively through various exercises. The training site included a series of dimly lit underground bunkers. Each of the dogs was given a human odor to track and then sent into the maze of bunkers. If successful, the dog would come upon a man in a bite suit. The dog's reward would be several minutes of aggressive biting, until called off by his handler. I had already witnessed Balto and Falco performing these feats under harrowing conditions. It no longer surprised me that dogs could track so swiftly and attack so aggressively. Still, it was impressive to see them learning their craft when they were just youngsters.

I can recall only one of the dogs being difficult to handle (he was later dismissed from the SEAL program and found a home in law enforcement). They were mostly well behaved and eager to work. But there were two dogs that stood out from the pack. One was named Bronco; the other was named Cairo. In both personality and performance, they were awesome dogs!

We met the dogs briefly. Like I said, there wasn't a lot of petting or messing around. But we did get an opportunity to let the dogs walk among us, sniff us, and see how they would react to us. I gravitated toward Cairo, mainly because of the way he looked and how well he performed in the training exercises. I also really liked Bronco. He was the more outwardly friendly of the two. He nudged up against me and almost seemed like he wanted to play. Cairo was a little more laid-back; not unfriendly, but more serious about working. I liked them both, but I leaned slightly toward Bronco as my top choice.

For the next two weeks, we got to know the new team of dogs in a hands-on setting. With each new day, we would spend more time interacting with the dogs. A lot of it was simple leash work: teaching the dog to walk at a certain pace and to obey basic commands.

This was not just for the dog's benefit. It was for our benefit. These animals had already spent two to three years being trained at a high level. Their SEAL handlers, on the other hand, had almost no experience with dog training. So we started with baby steps, walking around the kennel with a dog on a leash, instructing him to heel or sit. Then we'd take him off leash and allow him to do what he was bred and trained to do: run, smell, detect.

We used a lot of different equipment in training, including an electronic collar (sometimes referred to as an "e-collar" or "shock collar"). This is a device that might seem unnecessary or even cruel. But on a dangerous mission, it can save a dog's life.

These are smart, complex animals with a fierce desire to track and hunt prey. Sometimes, the only way to get the dog to let go, or to return to a safe spot, is to give him a little zap with the e-collar. If that sounds unkind, well, it sure beats the alternative: a fatally wounded dog. I found the e-collar to be a safe and effective training tool. The amount of electricity generated is minimal. It's harmless and causes no pain or damage to the dog. It just gets his attention. And that can often save his life.

Ideally you wouldn't have to use the e-collar. You'd just yell "*Los!*" which means "let go" or "release." Most of these commands the dogs had heard since they were puppies undergoing early training in Europe. In terms of communication, we had a good foundation on which to build. If we were playing fetch, the dog would race to pick up a toy or a ball and bring it back to me. Then he would sometimes refuse to let go. He would want to play tug-of-war with the toy or ball. To get him to drop, I would say "*Los!*" If he let go, he would be rewarded with a ball or words of encouragement (or both). If he didn't . . . he'd get nothing. And then we'd do it again.

This was the foundation of all training: convincing the dog to work in such a manner that he would receive positive reinforcement. A working dog needs to work, and he wants nothing more than to please his handler . . . his master . . .

his *dad.* And there was no more important or more commonly used command than *Los!*

We all learned the second language of MWD training, which includes dozens of commands used to convey a variety of instructions. The commands are important. But so is the manner in which they are delivered.

Obviously, we didn't learn all the commands right away. But we were introduced to the basic language of being a dog handler. I found it fascinating.

Each handler worked with multiple dogs each day. Before long I could see that Cairo was exceptional. I began to have doubts about my choice. I still liked Bronco. A lot. He was such a fun dog to be around. But I could tell Cairo was going to be a great dog to work with. I felt like he could teach me as much as I could teach him. I was really torn.

As the end of our two-week indoctrination period drew near, I started to wonder which dog would be assigned to me. All the new handlers would soon be leaving with their dogs for a much longer training school in California. I had expressed an interest in both Bronco and Cairo, but I never said, explicitly, "I want Bronco" or "I want Cairo." And no one asked. The trainers knew a lot more about dogs than I did, so I trusted their judgment. They watched all of us work with the dogs for two weeks, and in the end made the assignments they felt were appropriate.

"You're getting Cairo," Jim Hagerty said to me. "He's the right dog for you."

I shrugged. "Okay, cool."

At the time, I'm not sure I agreed with Jim's decision. But I was satisfied with the assignment. I liked Cairo a lot. I knew he was a great working dog and probably would be an easier dog to train than Bronco. I just liked that Bronco seemed a bit more playful when I first met him.

I later realized I had misjudged Cairo. He was not just friendly and affectionate but as loyal and loving a dog as you could ever hope to find. It took a little time to peel away the layers, but he was well worth the effort.

CHAPTER 8

Just a few short days after Cairo was assigned to me (and I was assigned to him), we flew to Southern California for seven weeks of intensive training. Most of the new dogs and their handlers made this trip. It was an opportunity to bond and work on the skills we would use when we went on missions together.

But let's be clear about one thing: When we arrived in Southern California, I needed just as much training as Cairo. Maybe more.

The training was intense and nonstop. Cairo became my roommate, training partner, and best friend. And it happened almost immediately. The navy handed me the reins one morning in Virginia, and suddenly Cairo was my full-time responsibility. We would live together, work together, sleep together, and sometimes even eat together.

I was no stranger to the close relationship between man and dog. I'd had dogs before and even had a pet Doberman at the time I became a dog handler. I was totally comfortable around dogs and liked spending time with them. But this was different. Cairo wasn't just a "dog." He was a finely tuned instrument. He was a model of exceptional breeding and training who was now being groomed for some of the most vital work in the US military.

For me, and for Cairo, it was an awesome responsibility. Not that he noticed.

We trained at a facility owned and operated by Adlerhorst International, the same company that had sponsored the European trip on which Cairo was purchased. Very early in our time together, I took Cairo to one of the training sessions. We drove in a small sport utility vehicle (SUV) from our hotel to the training site. The parking lot was filled with trucks and SUVs, all with their windows down or liftgates raised, and portable kennels in the back. I lifted the hatch so that Cairo would have plenty of air, told him I'd be back in a little while. Then I went inside for the classroom portion of the session.

The days were often broken down in this manner: an hour or two of classroom instruction, followed by practical training for the handler and his dog. Well, when I went back outside to the car, I noticed the door to the kennel was . . . missing. It had been completely blown off and was lying on the ground some six feet away from the truck. Cairo was gone!

A thousand horrible scenarios ran through my head. I worried that a seventy-pound attack dog—a purebred fighting machine—was loose in the area and might run into another dog, or some unsuspecting civilian.

A few minutes passed as I searched the area and called out for Cairo. There was no response. Eventually I made my way back to the car. I was angry at Cairo for breaking out, but even angrier at myself for not being more careful.

When I got to the car, I was shocked by what I found. There was Cairo, sitting quietly in his kennel. As I drew near, I stifled the urge to yell at him for breaking out. After all, it wasn't really his fault. And anyway, scolding a dog long after the infraction does nothing but confuse the poor guy. If I had yelled at Cairo in that moment as he sat in his kennel, lightly wagging his tail, he would have assumed that merely sitting there was some sort of correctable offense. Which, of course, it was not. So instead,

I swallowed my anger and embarrassment, gave him a pat on the head, and pulled him out of the kennel.

"Let's get to work, buddy."

So . . . what happened? I can only guess. Knowing Cairo the way I do now, I imagine he felt the call of nature and decided to bust out of his kennel. He was strong enough and smart enough to do that. Once he'd finished going to the bathroom, he was also smart and reliable enough to jump right back into his kennel. He then waited patiently for his handler to return. I just hadn't seen him because he was deep in the back of the kennel. The door gate was missing, so I thought he was still out running around somewhere.

When I reached in and patted his head, Cairo simply panted and gave me a look that seemed to say *Where you been, Dad?*

I took no chances with Cairo around other people, especially in the beginning. When I brought him back to the hotel after a day of training, I'd go straight to my room. If we had to walk through the lobby, I'd make sure he was harnessed and leashed, and usually tightly muzzled. As Cairo grew older, this would no longer be necessary. But for now, I handled him with a lot of respect and caution.

Once in our room, I'd let Cairo have the run of the place. On the first night in California he slept in his kennel. By the second night we were sharing a bed. I can even recall push-ing him off in the middle of the night for hogging all the blankets! This was a pattern throughout our time together. With some dogs, boundaries are critical. They must know their place. If you let them on your bed, or the couch, they won't respect your authority or understand their place in the "pack." If you try to push them away, they will growl unhap-pily. It's a sign of dominance. A dog handler must be careful about letting this behavior go unchecked.

Fortunately, this was not the case with Cairo. He just liked sleeping on a bed rather than in his kennel or on the floor. And he liked curling up next to his dad. It strengthened our bond.

While Cairo was a tireless worker during the day, he was laid-back in the evening. We'd sit together on the couch and watch TV. It was almost like hanging out with one of my buddies. As with many close friendships, I almost felt like I could read Cairo's mind.

The days in California were filled with exercises in scent detection, bite work, command response, desensitization to sound, and physical training. It was a lot like what we had done in Virginia, but in much greater depth.

I put on the bite suit and felt the power of these dogs firsthand. It was, to say the least, impressive! At seventy pounds, they were less than half my size. But getting hit by one of these animals, when running at full speed, was like being thrown into a wall. We had to be careful to avoid injury. The dog was doing what came naturally to him. It was up to the handler to help him remain safe during instruction. He did this by "catching" the dog and pulling him in for the bite.

Despite the padding, most handlers finished the course with purple welts all over their arms and legs. I didn't mind. The bruises were daily reminders of the awesome power of Cairo and his fellow working dogs.

It should be noted that I never wore the bite suit while working with Cairo, only while working with other dogs. A rule of training MWDs is that you never allow your own dog to bite you. The dog must remember that his personal handler is the boss.

When Cairo was learning to attack and bite, my role was to supervise. As Cairo wrestled with a flailing target, I'd hook my hip leash to his harness and give him a pat on the ribs or on the top of his head. I was always careful not to interfere with his mouth when he was in attack mode.

"Good boy," was my first response. It indicated to Cairo that he had followed orders, and that we were in this thing together. We were a team. His job was to find and bite; mine was to reward him afterward and let him know that he could safely release the target. Most dogs are usually reluctant to give up a bite, and Cairo was no different. I'd praise him for a job well done and gently pull up on his collar. The last thing I wanted to do was choke my own dog, not only because it would hurt him but also because he would think he was being punished.

This would confuse him:

"Wait, you just told me good job for biting this guy, but now you're choking me because I won't let go?! What's up with that, Dad? Make up your mind!"

If I lifted the collar at the right angle, I could apply just enough pressure to loosen his jaws. This would cause him to drop the target. Then I'd give him another pat or even a quick hug.

"Good job, buddy."

I would do everything possible to make sure that Cairo found the experience to be a positive one. And no matter how well I knew him, and how much I thought he respected me, I would never put my hands near his mouth when he was on a bite. Release was always achieved through easily under-stood commands and effective collar pressure, coupled with common sense and patience. By the time we left California, I could usually convince Cairo to return from an attack with-out even touching him. Most of the dogs were pretty good about that.

Cairo was exceptional.

The entire California trip was a great experience. It made me a much better handler and Cairo a better working dog. It really brought us closer together.

At the end of the seven-week program, there was a com-petition involving the dogs and their handlers. We were put through exercises and given scores. In one of the events, we had to paddle across a pond together in a light canoe. What we didn't know is that when we were halfway across the water, a man in a bite suit would jump out from behind some rocks and begin shouting. Several of the dogs got excited and cap-sized their boats. Not Cairo. He sat calmly and waited until he was told what to do.

We ended up finishing second in the competition. We got caught right at the end by another SEAL, a guy from a dif-ferent squadron. But it wasn't Cairo's fault. It was all on me. I was just a little slow. As usual, Cairo did his job.

CHAPTER 9

Cairo might have been better at skydiving than I was. I mean, he never jumped on a mission, simply because he didn't have to. More often than not we would land by chopper and hike to the target. Or we would fast rope from twenty to fifty or even one hundred feet overhead. But he jumped in training. A lot. And he was as cool as could be.

When we finished the program in California, we returned to Virginia for more training, and to prepare for our next deployment. We would take trips to various sites to work on different aspects of training. For example, we'd go to Arizona to work on skydiving for a couple of weeks at a time.

Of all the things I learned to do as a SEAL, skydiving

was probably the most challenging. Not because of the fear factor. I had a summer construction job in high school that involved climbing utility poles. That made my knees weak. But for some reason I didn't mind jumping out of a plane.

That might sound strange, but it actually makes sense. When you're only a few stories above the ground, everything looks real. And yet, just distant enough to envision the damage that will be done if you fall. But from ten thousand feet, the earth seems distant and almost unreal.

I rarely felt any butterflies in my stomach when skydiving. Over the course of my navy career, I made at least three hundred jumps, nearly all of them during training exercises. I became competent enough that I never caused any problems or suffered any injuries. But it was not my strong suit. I knew some SEALs who were extraordinary skydivers, with thousands of jumps to their credit. They loved it! Didn't matter if it was day or night, windy or calm. These guys just wanted to jump. They were the ones you wanted leading a string of guys out the back of a plane.

One of the reasons I regret not becoming more skilled at skydiving is because I never got the opportunity to jump with Cairo. The dogs, as I said, did not jump alone. They were muzzled, harnessed, and tucked safely into a big pouch (almost like a baby carrier) worn by a human skydiver. Together they would float to earth under a huge canopy.

The dog carrier was always one of the strongest jumpers in the unit. For this exercise, skydiving skill was more important than dog-handling experience. Some dogs found the experience terrifying. That's why their handler would apply a muzzle and darkened goggles ("doggles") before the jump. He wanted to limit the dog's visibility to prevent him from panicking.

Most of the dogs that were good enough to be in a Special Operations unit like the SEALs seemed to almost enjoy the skydiving experience. Cairo fell into that category. I'd load him into the pouch of a more seasoned jumper, attach his muzzle and doggles, and give him a big pat on the head before each jump. A few second later, we would both be on our way. Sometimes I'd look up and get a glimpse of him floating gently above me. I could almost see him smiling. He never freaked out. Not once.

For the next six months, from December of 2008 to June of 2009, Cairo and I were virtually inseparable. We spent all our time training for our first deployment together. Military working dogs resided in kennels on the base, but Cairo often came home with me at the end of the day. This was frowned upon, but usually ignored. Everyone understood the importance of a handler bonding with his dog. What better way to do that than by taking Cairo home and splitting a steak with him?

The training was challenging. I discovered quickly that Cairo preferred bite work to almost any other aspect of training. From our perspective, odor detection was the most important skill a dog could possess. The ability to sniff out weapons or explosives could save dozens of lives on a mission. To Cairo, though, the reward for scent detection (a hug or a pat on the head, or even a treat) was far less satisfying than the rewards associated with tracking a target.

A bite.

Cairo was friendly and playful, even around strangers. But he was still an attack dog. Centuries of breeding, combined with the best training money could buy, had made him a highly adept hunter. Nothing made him happier than to sink his teeth into his prey. That's just a simple fact.

This was especially true as he became more seasoned. Therefore, it was important to work regularly on scent detection and find new ways to make the training interesting and fun.

At home, I would frequently take Cairo to the beach and work on odor detection with him. On training trips, it was a little more challenging. In Arizona, for example, we'd do a full day of skydiving. Then, even if we were both exhausted, I'd make sure we got in some scent work. Once in a while, as a reward for good odor detection work, I'd let him go after someone in a bite suit. For both of us, the bite work was more fun, but the scent work was more important. It was also a skill that deteriorated swiftly, so I tried to stay on top of it.

I worked Cairo hard because it was my job, but also because he was unhappy if he didn't get enough exercise. Any working dog will make your life miserable if you don't respect his genetic makeup. When I was a little kid, we had a Siberian husky. His name was Smokey. This name was appropriate because most of the time he ran around like his fur was on fire! I played with Smokey a lot, but I always ran out of gas before he did.

I remember one day he literally pulled a tree out of the ground. It wasn't a huge tree, but neither was it a little weed. Nope. It was a real tree, maybe ten feet tall, with a narrow trunk and low-hanging branches. Well, one morning Smokey started digging around the base of the tree. He pawed and shoveled like a maniac. I sat out on the porch and watched with amazement as he dug frantically for hours.

Every so often he would stop digging, rest for a bit, and then begin tugging on the tree. He'd wrap his jaws around the slender trunk and pull. Then he'd jump up and grab one of the branches and pull on that. Pretty soon the tree was bent over at a 45-degree angle. Then a 90-degree angle. At one point I went outside and tried to coax Smokey away from the tree, figuring he'd have a heart attack if he kept it up much longer. But he would not quit because, well, he was a husky. He was bred to run and fight.

Eventually, Smokey's effort was rewarded. The tree wiggled like a loose tooth and began to give up its roots. I remember being amazed at how much of the tree had been hidden beneath the surface: a couple of feet of tendrils, caked with dirt and debris.

When it was over, I ran over to give Smokey a hug, but he wasn't all that enthusiastic. He sniffed at the roots, then walked away and took a well-deserved nap.

That is what it's like to own any type of working dog. You have to know what you are getting into. And you must be willing to put in the time to properly train him. Otherwise, you will both be unhappy.

Cairo was a military working dog, bred and trained to be part of a SEAL team. He needed to work, and so I worked him. At least twice a day I'd let him run until he'd had enough. In the springtime, we spent less time at the beach and more time training on less forgiving surfaces: concrete, pavement, rocky hillsides, and mountains. Military working dogs don't wear boots, after all (booties are available, but the dogs hate them!). So Cairo had to get accustomed to the rough terrain he would face in the mountains of Afghanistan.

This kind of training can be unpleasant, but Cairo was such a happy and energetic dog that he soon adjusted. We'd run together on sidewalks and rutted trails. We'd play fetch in parking lots. Slowly but surely, Cairo began to develop calluses on his pads—thick, crusty shields that would protect him against the brutal terrain he was soon to face.

By the end of May he was ready for his first deployment.

And I couldn't wait to see him in action.

CHAPTER 10

Cairo and I arrived at Forward Operating Base Sharana, in the highlands of Paktika Province, Afghanistan, in June of 2009.

Sharana was one of the largest US military bases in Afghanistan before it was closed in 2013 and returned to the Afghan government. Approximately thirty to forty members of our squadron were stationed at Sharana, along with support personnel. We shared a dining hall with the regular troops but had our own living quarters. The squadron was divided into two separate huts.

Cairo slept right alongside us. It was a big, well-appointed camp, but there were no designated kennels built for the dogs. This wasn't a big deal because we only had two dogs at this location. I stayed in one hut with Cairo, while the other dog and his handler stayed in a different hut. This lessened the chance that the dogs might get into a disagreement (a turf war, so to speak). It also reduced the impact of their presence on the other members of the team.

The huts were divided into small, individual sleeping sections for each member of the team, along with a big area at the end of the hut for relaxing and hanging out when we weren't working. The living area was furnished with couches, a refrigerator, an ice machine, and a television.

I kept a small kennel in the living area for Cairo to sleep in, but he was just as likely to share my quarters. Since the sleeping rooms were tiny, they accommodated only a twin bed, which was raised off the floor to create additional space. Cairo would usually sleep on a rug, although sometimes he'd try to jump up on the bed. At home, where I had a queen-sized bed, I didn't mind. But sharing a twin mattress with a full-grown Malinois?

Sorry, Cairo. Gotta draw the line somewhere.

Our first deployment together was a busy four-month assignment. We would go out on missions five or six times a week. A typical mission would begin with locating a target.

A "target" might be a person, or a group of people, or a structure that was used to hide weapons. We would outline the whole mission at a briefing. We would talk about the identity of the target and the responsibility of each of the two teams in the squadron.

I would get together with the other dog handler and team leaders, and together we would decide who would support each of the teams. Then we would each brief our team about the dog and its capabilities and the gear we would be carrying. By the end of a deployment, most of this information was old news to the rest of the team. But we shared it anyway, every night.

If a chaplain was available, the briefing ended with a prayer. Then we would swing into action. Each operator would go to the "ready room" to prepare his personal gear. (The ready room was a separate building where we kept our equipment in cubbies, packed and ready to go, so that we could embark on a moment's notice.)

My first responsibility was to check my weapons and be certain that they were functioning properly. Then I'd go through a mental checklist of supplies. These included fresh batteries in my night vision goggles, enough water for me and Cairo, and a fully functioning radio. Then I'd check all of Cairo's gear, most of which was located on his vest. And of course, I would check to make sure his e-collar was functioning properly. I also carried a small, collapsible bowl to give Cairo water on patrol and a medical kit designed to treat canine injuries.

In every way, Cairo was one of the guys. Except he was a dog, which by nature made him somewhat unpredictable. We were only a few days into the deployment when we went out on our first operation—looking for bad guys.

Usually we would bring two dogs on each mission: one positioned at the front of the patrol, the other in the middle. On this night, Cairo and I were at the front. I remember feeling excited as we hiked in. This was my fourth deployment as a Navy SEAL, and my second to Afghanistan. Although each mission was unique, I knew basically what to expect.

And yet, the fact that I had a full-grown Belgian Malinois by my side added a layer of excitement. In some ways, I felt like I was starting all over. I knew there was a good chance the night would end with a fight. It often did. But my job would be different than it had been in the past.

I was a dog handler, and my first responsibility was to take care of Cairo. And to make sure that he did the job for which he had been trained. This was his first mission. I wondered how he would do, and how I would do as a handler. If Cairo messed up, it was not merely a reflection on me but a danger to everyone in the squadron.

I controlled Cairo with my hip lead. A hip lead is a leash that runs from the dog's harness to his handler's belt. This allowed me to keep my hands free to hold a weapon. We walked across a moonlit field toward a small compound. Cairo seemed comfortable in his surroundings. I wondered if he had any idea that this was not an exercise but rather the real deal.

We entered the compound and crossed a courtyard. To my surprise, we encountered a herd of a few dozen sheep. This could have been a bloody disaster. In all our months of training, one thing we had not simulated was a courtyard filled with farm animals. Cairo had chased down hundreds of bad guys in bite suits. He had detected explosives in fields and darkened movie theaters. He had jumped out of planes and calmly crossed a lake in a canoe.

He had been nearly perfect.

But he had never been presented with a scenario in which dozens of helpless, crying little animals stood between him and the successful completion of his task. There was no way of knowing how he would respond.

I heard a voice whisper from behind me.

"You got him, Cheese?"

(Cheese was my nickname.)

I nodded, even though I wasn't sure I had anything.

As the sheep began to bleat, I reached down and grabbed Cairo by the harness. Immediately, he stopped in his tracks.

What's wrong, Dad?

Without speaking, I scooped up Cairo and tossed him over my shoulder like a sack of laundry.

Cairo was in full "hunt" mode. The last thing we needed was for him to be distracted by a herd of crying sheep. I had no idea how he might react to being suddenly withdrawn from his usual position. In training, I had never encountered a situation like this. Cairo could have barked and yelped. He could have struggled to jump out of my arms. It was also possible that if I had left him on the ground, he would have walked right past the little critters.

I couldn't take any chances. Cairo was an attack dog. A highly trained and even-tempered attack dog, yes. But he was still an attack dog. I figured that given half a chance, he might see the sheep as a midnight snack.

Cairo, however, was as cool as could be. He didn't try to wrestle away from me. As we stepped quietly through the herd, his body pressed against my back, he just looked at the sheep with curiosity until they were out of sight. Then I put him down, gave him a firm but approving pat on the head, and let him go back to work.

As it turned out, that was the highlight of the evening. There were no bites, no bad guys, no explosives . . . nothing. As often happened in Afghanistan, this particular hole was dry. Or, at least, it was dry by the time we arrived.

Nevertheless, I considered the mission to be a success. It reminded me that despite our training, it was impossible to plan for everything. There would always be surprises. But Cairo had done his job perfectly. When faced with a serious distraction, he had merely shrugged.

What more could you ask of the guy?

Cairo had passed the first test. He was now officially a member of the squadron.

Cairo never ceased to amaze me. On many missions our objective was to capture or eliminate a target. This was intense, dangerous work. The missions were often complicated by the presence of not just unexpected wildlife but civilians. More than once I held my breath as Cairo raced into a building in search of an enemy fighter. I never knew what the outcome might be.

When Cairo got his very first bite, I was startled by the damage it did. The bad guy had nearly lost his arm while struggling to get free of Cairo (he was lucky to survive). But even more surprising was the sight of a tiny, bundled baby not far from where the man had been hiding.

To get to his target, Cairo must have run right past the infant. Considering his extraordinary sense of smell, he surely would have stopped to investigate. I don't quite know how to explain the fact that he didn't harm the child, except to say that Cairo was indeed a special dog.

He knew right from wrong.

He knew good from bad.

CHAPTER 11

Cairo was one of the boys.

He lived with us, ate with us, slept with us, played with us, trained with us, and fought with us. Sometimes he even pranked with us.

On July 29, 2009, I woke early in the afternoon. This wasn't unusual, as we'd been out on a mission the night before and would be going out again on this night. You learn to sleep almost anywhere in the military, and to nod off on a moment's notice. I've seen men snoring their way through a loud and bumpy chopper ride into a drop zone. I've seen guys go from a dead sleep to a firefight in a matter of seconds.

It's amazing what the mind can do under the right circumstances.

On this day, I woke to the sight of Cairo wandering anxiously around the hut, breathing heavily. He gave me a look that was instantly recognizable as guilt.

"What's up, buddy?"

Cairo whimpered a little and kept walking. I went into a corner of the hut to retrieve my boots and found them practically swimming in a puddle of liquid. The smell, pungent and fresh, left no doubt as to the source. Cairo had peed in my boots.

"What the heck, dude?"

I hooked him up to a leash and led him outside, where Cairo quickly lifted a leg. But he managed only a dribble. No surprise. After the flood he'd left indoors, there couldn't have been much left in the system! I stood there for a moment looking at Cairo. He was such a reliable and well-trained dog. Honestly, I couldn't recall him ever having an accident like this. Bad enough that he peed all over our living quarters, but to do it in my boots?

I wondered for a moment. Was it really an accident? I mean, obviously the poor guy had to relieve himself. Ordinarily, if he had to go during the night (or whenever I was sleeping), he would just whimper a bit and I'd wake up and let him out. This time I must have slept through the alarm. Maybe he was unhappy and wanted to send a message by decorating my boots.

Like I said, a prankster.

Or maybe he was just looking for a familiar and friendly smell.

When we got back in the hut, I decided to have some fun with Cairo. After all, he was one of the boys. We were always playing jokes on one another.

"You're gonna mess with my feet, I'll mess with yours," I said. "Let's do a little booty work."

"Booty work" meant the application of small boots over a dog's paws. As noted earlier, I didn't often use these with Cairo. But sometimes the terrain was jagged or littered with broken glass. On those occasions, booties were a temporary precaution. Some dogs adapted to the booties better than others. Cairo preferred to go natural. He hated the booties, so I rarely forced him to wear them.

But I was a little grumpy now and figured some booty training would be a fitting but harmless punishment for peeing in my boots. As usual, he fought while I tried to put them on. Then he walked about the hut gingerly, as if tiptoeing across a hot beach. Watching him, I started to laugh. He was so cute! He would take a step forward, then two quick steps back. Then two steps forward, and one step back, like a little cat dance.

I grabbed a pair of doggles and strapped them loosely to Cairo's head. And then a pair of earmuffs—the kind we'd wear to protect ourselves from the roar of explosives. I snapped a few pictures while laughing so hard I could barely breathe. He actually looked like a canine superhero, all dressed up like that.

At that moment, a couple of guys from the team walked into the hut.

"Cheese, what are you doing?"

"Just having some fun with Cairo," I said, laughing. "He peed in my boots."

"Ah, come on, man."

They were both trying hard to stifle laughs as Cairo lurched about. But they were right. Even though Cairo was one of the boys, I knew better than to use him for our amusement. So I stripped off the glasses and booties and earmuffs and gave him a big hug.

"All right, pal. Sorry about that. I know you didn't mean it. My fault, anyway."

I led Cairo outside with some of the other guys and we took turns working him in a long and tiring game of fetch. I still have pictures of Cairo from that day, doing his superhero cat dance in the hut.

They always make me smile.

CHAPTER 12

A few hours later I boarded a helicopter with Cairo for the next mission. We had received intelligence about a target where explosives were being manufactured.

As we drew near, I could see a group of four men running from the building. They split into two groups and hopped onto motorcycles. Each motorcycle was weighed down with what appeared to be weapons.

But we had to be sure. We had to be 100 percent certain that these were grown men, and not boys who had been forced into the terrorist ranks. We had to be 100 percent certain they were really carrying RPGs and IEDs. We had to be 100 percent certain there were no civilians in the vicinity.

One hundred percent certainty. On all counts.

The only way to do this was to put the chopper down and pursue the men on foot.

One of the motorcycles made it to a cluster of trees near the top of a hill. The two passengers jumped off, grabbed some gear, and ran away. We set the helicopter down as close as we could to the tree line and went after them. This was risky, as we knew the insurgents were armed. They also had the high ground, which was a tactical advantage. But we had no other option. We weren't going to just let them get away.

I worked Cairo from the far right, into the wind. I figured he'd pick up the scent of the bad guys and work his way upwind to their hiding spot. But we couldn't just walk blindly into the trees. In this kind of scenario, a working dog is very important. You let him pick up the scent and then send him in to pinpoint the enemy's position, or to flush them out. If this sounds like dangerous work for the dog, well, it is.

As I led Cairo into the wind on a hip lead, he lifted his snout in excitement. I made my way to our team leader, Daniel.

"He's got it," I said. "We can send him in anytime."

Daniel nodded. "Okay. Whenever you're ready."

I unhooked Cairo's lead and gave him a pat on the behind.

He raced toward the tree line and quickly picked up on an odor. I'd seen Cairo do this dozens of times, but it never failed to impress. Oddly, there was a low concrete wall next to the tree line. Cairo easily hopped the barrier and continued working.

Cairo continued to follow the scent. For a while I could see him weaving in and out of the trees, but as Cairo got farther away, he faded from view. He was on the far left of the tree line while I was on the right, closest to our team leader.

Suddenly, I heard gunfire.

"Cairo!" I yelled. "*Los!*"

Even if I couldn't see what was happening, gunfire was a signal to retrieve the dog. The best-case scenario was that our team had found the bad guys and were in the thick of a firefight. And we'd probably win that fight. But there was no benefit to having Cairo in the way once bullets started flying. His presence was a distraction to the team. And he was in danger.

I said his name again. Then I gave him a quick hit with the e-collar and began moving toward the left end of the tree line. A dog handler's job in this situation is complicated. He is an operator. He is expected to fight. But he is also responsible for the safety of the team's dog. I hit the e-collar again.

"Cairo! Los!"

I continued to move. As I looked to my left, I could see the muzzle flash of gunfire coming from above the ground, apparently in the trees. And I could see our guys returning fire.

I continued to call for Cairo while holding my rifle chest high. I'm not sure how much time passed, but as the minutes went by, it became clear that something had happened to Cairo. He was a smart and obedient dog. Even when locked into a bite, he responded well to the e-collar. Given the intensity of the fight and the amount of gunfire, I began to worry that something terrible had happened.

"Cairo!" I repeated, still moving upwind along the trees. "Come on, buddy! Los!"

Finally, in the distance, I saw something moving. It was Cairo!

He emerged from the trees approximately thirty or forty meters away. I called his name again, this time loud enough to be heard through the night air, above the crack of gunfire. Everything was happening so fast, and yet time seemed to stand still. I watched as Cairo walked toward me. I was struck by the fact that he was not running but rather lurching awkwardly. Still, he followed my voice, my scent.

I ran to him as quickly as I could, but he fell to the ground just a few feet before I reached him. And he didn't just stop and lie down; he basically tipped over in midstride.

Oh no . . . he's dead.

It was as terrible and simple as that. I didn't have time to mourn. I couldn't afford to panic or lose focus. The stakes were too high. We still had a mission to accomplish, and now Cairo was no longer a part of that mission. He was gone.

Or so it seemed.

I knelt beside him as the gunfire ebbed. Under a moonlit sky, I could see that Cairo's fur was wet and matted with something dark. His eyes were slits, his breathing labored. Experience told me that the battle was over, or at least under control. We had more than a dozen men; they had two. It was now mop-up time, and my responsibility was to Cairo. I ran a hand along his vest, felt a hole soaked with something sticky. I patted him on the head.

"Hang in there, boy."

It seemed a miracle that Cairo was still alive. When a dog was wounded, it usually happened at point-blank range, and the dog rarely survived. But Cairo was tough. Or lucky. Or both, I guess.

As I stayed with Cairo, another member of the team peeled off and made his way back to us. Word had already come over the radio that we had suffered a FWIA—"friendly wounded in action." This is the worst thing you want to hear during or after a fight, and the fact that the "friendly" was a dog was no consolation. Cairo was part of the team. He was one of us.

The guy who had come back to help was a former combat medic. He immediately went into action, treating Cairo with just as much urgency as if he were a human. I removed Cairo's vest and handed the medic my canine medical kit. Then I gently slipped Cairo's muzzle over his snout. He was surely in a lot of pain. We didn't want to take a chance on him biting while we tried to treat him.

"We'll fix you up, Cairo," the medic said. "Don't worry."

Cairo barely reacted as the medic ripped open packages of gauze and stuffed them into his chest wound. One after another, deeper and deeper, his fingers disappearing into the hole. There was so much blood, so much damage. At one point, as the medic rooted around, trying to stem the flow of blood, Cairo yelped and turned his head. The muzzle smacked against the medic's hand.

"Sorry," he said.

I rubbed a hand along Cairo's back, trying to calm him down. The medic stabilized Cairo's chest wound. Then he began gently moving his hands around Cairo's entire body. By now he was covered in blood, and we didn't have much light, so it was hard to tell whether there were any other wounds. As it turned out, there were. Another bullet had hit Cairo in the right foreleg. Must have hurt like crazy, but compared to the chest wound, it was a minor concern. In humans or canines, battlefield chest wounds are very bad, and often fatal.

Within a few minutes, a medevac helicopter was called in. I boarded with Cairo, along with the medic, and we flew back to Sharana, where a team of doctors worked on him for nearly two hours. And when I say doctors, I mean *physicians*. The kind who treat human soldiers. See, there were no veterinarians at Sharana, so Cairo was treated just like any other wounded member of the US armed forces. The doctors performed an emergency tracheotomy to clear his airway so that he wouldn't drown in his own blood. They inserted chest tubes. They put a brace on his leg to stabilize that wound and to keep his femur from falling apart.

They saved his life.

And the night wasn't over yet. As soon as Cairo was out of immediate danger, he was put on a plane bound for Bagram Airfield, the closest military base with a veterinary staff. Bagram was the granddaddy of all US bases in Afghanistan. The staff there was equipped to deal with a wide variety of medical issues, including those pertaining to working dogs. Technically speaking, I didn't have to make the trip with him. There were other experienced dog handlers at Bagram.

I went because Cairo was my dog. I wanted to be with him.

It wasn't unusual for the details of a particular mission to trickle out slowly. Hours or even days could pass before a clear picture was presented. I later found out that Cairo had performed heroically. He had saved lives and impacted the mission.

Here's what happened:

As Cairo followed the scent between the wall and the tree line, he came upon the two bad guys. One of them was on the ground, using a flashlight in an attempt to misdirect us and draw us closer. The second guy was in a tree, hiding in some lower branches. As Cairo engaged the guy on the ground, the other guy began shooting at Cairo from above. Two of the bullets struck Cairo, one in the chest, one in the leg. This ended the battle for Cairo. It also revealed the insurgents' position, which allowed our soldiers to move in and control the fight.

As soon as the gunfire started, I had called out to Cairo and punched his e-collar to get him to come home. He did exactly as he was told, despite being gravely wounded. Unable to jump back over the wall because of his injuries, Cairo had to go all the way around it in order to make his way back to me. I had no idea what was happening to him at the time. I just kept calling him and buzzing him. And he made it. With a shattered leg and a gaping chest wound, Cairo staggered home to Dad.

So, yeah, I accompanied him to Sharana, and then to Bagram. It was the least I could do.

CHAPTER 13

I spent the night on the floor of Cairo's room in the veterinary hospital at Bagram. He looked to be in a world of hurt, although I don't think he was aware of much in those first few hours. He had bandages on his chest and a cast on his right foreleg. (The cast was later signed by the veterinarians and staff who had inserted a metal plate in his leg.) His face and body were bloated from steroids and intravenous liquids.

The poor guy looked exactly like what he was: a wounded warrior.

I was too worried to sleep much that night. If something happened to Cairo, I wanted to be alert so that I could call his treatment team right away. And if he died, I wanted my face to be the last thing he saw. I wanted to hold him close and tell him how much I loved him. I wanted him to know how much everyone on the team respected him and appreciated his sacrifice. He deserved at least that much.

As the night went on, I inched closer to Cairo's swollen torso and gently rubbed the back of his head. I told him again what a great job he had done and how proud of him I was. Over the course of the previous year, I'd spent a lot of nights nudging Cairo off the bed or pulling blankets away from him so that I could get a decent night's sleep. But right now, on the cold tile of a hospital recovery room, I just wanted to keep him close. I stayed right by his side, just as he would have stayed by my side if the situation had been reversed.

Still sedated by anesthesia and painkillers, Cairo seemed unaware of his surroundings. His breathing was shallow. The medical staff had done a great job patching him up, but I still couldn't help but wonder whether he'd pull through. It was a miracle that he'd even made it this far. This was a sad fact of military life: When a dog was engaged by an armed insurgent, the result was often fatal. For both of them. Bad guy shoots dog, good guys shoot bad guy. End of story.

But not this time.

By morning, Cairo had started to come around. His face

remained almost comically bloated, and he was clearly in pain. But when he opened his eyes and gave me a little lick, I knew he was getting better.

"Hey, buddy," I said, giving him a gentle rub on the the neck. "Welcome back."

Cairo burrowed into me and let out a little moan. Pretty soon the docs were in the room, checking him out, declaring his wounds to be clean and healing well. They were impressed by Cairo's toughness and durability.

"Hey, boy," one of the nurses said. "Let's try to get you on your feet."

Obviously, Cairo had no idea what she had said, but his expression indicated something along the lines of "Are you nuts?"

Together, very slowly, we helped him stand up. A day earlier he had been as healthy as could be—a fit and eager working dog going off on a mission. All MWDs are energetic, but Cairo was unique. He never seemed to tire. He could outwork all of us.

But now here he was, unable to take even a step without a couple of humans guiding him along the way. He gave me a sad look as he limped slowly forward, just a few inches at a time.

"You're doing great," I said. "I'm proud of you."

I thought he might not cover more than a few feet of ground in the recovery room, but I had underestimated him. As Cairo shuffled along, he seemed to gain confidence. His gait straightened. His pace quickened a bit. Don't get me wrong. Compared to his usual speed, Cairo was in slow motion. But the very fact that he was walking on his own was cause for celebration. Although the doctors advised cautious optimism, I couldn't help but feel as though he had weathered the storm.

"Yeah, you're going to be all right, aren't you, boy?"

His response was to continue walking—out of the room, down a hallway, and out the back door, where a large, open stretch of dirt and rocks awaited.

When it comes to recovering from surgery, the process for dogs is similar to humans in a few significant ways. In both cases, movement is important. Getting a patient up and out of bed promotes healing and a positive attitude. Cairo was walking. That was a good sign. Another good sign is when the patient demonstrates that his plumbing is working properly. A wounded soldier who can go to the bathroom is a patient on the way to recovery.

Cairo dropped his nose instinctively as he walked out into

the desert sun. I put a pair of sunglasses on his head to protect his puffy eyes from the glare. Then he went about the business of sniffing for an appropriate place to pee. It didn't take him long. I laughed and gave him another pat on the back.

"Good job, big guy!"

That first little walk took a lot out of Cairo. He went right back inside and took a long nap. By the next morning, the IV line had been removed and he walked with more of a bounce in his step. He also ate a small amount of food. When anyone said his name, his tail wagged. This was a sure sign that his mood had improved.

For three days, I barely left Cairo's side. My commanding officer and teammates were helpful. They understood my desire to stay with Cairo until he was stable. I hung out with him, took him for long, slow walks, and fed him by hand until he was able to eat on his own. I just wanted to let him know how much I cared.

It wasn't long before the doctors were confident that Cairo would make a full recovery. I wasn't sure what that meant. Cairo, after all, was a military working dog. That's what he was bred and trained to do. Making a "full recovery" didn't necessarily mean he would ever go on another mission.

"Will he work again?" I asked one of the docs.

He shrugged and smiled. "Hard to say. Maybe."

After three days of rehab, it was time to get back to work. For me, that meant flying to Sharana and rejoining my squadron. For Cairo, it meant a trip home.

Well, not exactly home. His destination was Lackland Air Force Base in Texas, site of the Department of Defense Military Working Dog Program. With more than sixty training areas and seven hundred kennels spread out over three thousand acres, Lackland is easily the largest MWD training center in the world. It is also home to the best canine medical care and rehabilitation facilities, which was exactly what Cairo needed.

The fact that he was going to Lackland was a good sign. He would be given every opportunity to resume his life as a member of the team. Selfishly, I hoped he would recover and return not just because he was a great working dog but because he was my partner.

Cairo was my dog, and I was his dad. If he were retired, I would miss him. The military tried to reunite handlers with their service dogs after the dogs' careers ended. But there was no guarantee. Especially since I was still an active dog handler. And even if Cairo's injuries were too severe for him to return to duty as a Special Operations canine, there were other jobs available. He could work for law enforcement as an odor detection specialist. He didn't have to be a superhero or even particularly athletic to sniff out explosives or drugs.

Cairo was only four years old. The military had invested tens of thousands of dollars in his care and training. He was worth every penny of that investment. Bum leg or not, there was still a place for him as a working dog. He was far too young to be sent out to pasture. The only question was, how badly was he damaged? At Lackland, there would be an answer.

Just three days after he was nearly killed on the battlefield, Cairo was airlifted out of Bagram on the first leg of a long journey to Texas. He was accompanied by a Master at Arms named Mike. This was actually the second half of Mike's assignment that week. The first part was to accompany another working dog from Virginia to Afghanistan. That dog was Bronco! The very same Malinois who had nearly become my dog during the initial assignment phase of training.

Mike and I hung around for a day, swapping stories and playing with the dogs. I had to become reacquainted with

Bronco, since I would be his handler for the remainder of the deployment (roughly two more months). And Mike, who loved dogs as much as I did, wanted to spend a little time with Cairo before taking him back to the States.

Late in the afternoon, I packed up Cairo's gear and loaded it onto the huge cargo plane that would carry him halfway around the world. Before putting him in his kennel for the trip, we posed for some photos. I asked Mike to take good care of Cairo. I promised to do the same for Bronco. I gave Cairo a hug and closed the door on his kennel.

"See you around, boy."

CHAPTER 14

Throughout the rest of the deployment, I got good reports on Cairo. His wounds had healed. He was doing well with rehab. He was in great hands at Lackland. But I wondered whether he would ever be fit enough to return to his role as an active duty military working dog.

Would he lose a step because of his shattered femur? Would he have trouble breathing because of his chest wound? And what about his mental state? Human soldiers often suffer from something called post-traumatic stress disorder (PTSD). They carry physical and emotional scars from their time in battle.

The same thing can happen to canines.

Cairo had been shot at point-blank range. We all knew men who had gone through exactly that same amount of trauma. Sometimes they returned to combat duty. Sometimes they did not. Same thing with dogs. When you get wounded, you're never quite the same. It's an illusion that SEALs are different. I mean, yeah, we're different. We have better training and perhaps a better ability to fight and not quit.

But the truth is . . . getting shot or blown up is terrible. Even if you're lucky enough to survive, it will mess you up—mentally as well as physically. It will change your life and the way you look at things. That is simply a fact. We aren't superheroes; neither was Cairo.

I got back from Afghanistan in October. Cairo was still in Texas, receiving world-class training and rehabilitation. I continued to receive good reports. The docs and trainers said he had made a nearly full recovery. There was no reason why he couldn't return to active duty. But what of his spirit? I wondered. What about his heart? Would he be the same dog I'd come to know and love? Would he be nervous or frightened? Would he have the same drive to work?

And what would happen if we deployed again? How

would he respond to bumpy helicopter flights in the middle of the night? Or to gunfire and explosions? Would he rush into a dark room with the same fearlessness he had exhibited in the past, or would he sit down and refuse to perform?

Hey, Dad . . . I really don't want to do this right now. I'm scared.

How would I respond? With compassion? Anger? The bottom line is this: If you can't do the job, then you shouldn't be on the mission. Lives are at stake. It's as simple as that.

Cairo didn't get a vote in any of this. He would be observed and tested, and if he appeared fit for duty, then he'd be back in the game. Time would tell.

A few weeks later, I got a phone call saying Cairo had returned to Virginia. I drove straight from my home to the kennel to see him. I wondered how he would react. Would he remember me? Would he be anxious? Would my presence trigger some sort of flashback to the worst night of his life?

I parked my truck and walked straight to the kennel. I didn't even stop at command to talk with any of the guys. Cairo saw me approaching from several yards away and began jumping around. The sound of his playful whimpering brought a smile to my face. I opened the gate, and he leaped into my chest. Cairo liked to greet me that way. He would stand on his hind legs and let me hold his forelegs in my hands or against my chest. The force of his enthusiasm nearly knocked me over.

I laughed. "Hey, buddy! How have you been?"

Cairo danced around me, jumping like a rodeo bronc, and butting me with his muzzle. I put a hand through his collar and pulled him close, let him breathe right in my face. His breath was terrible, as usual. I didn't care.

"It's okay, Cairo. Dad's back. Everything's going to be all right."

The dogs lived in a nice kennel on the base. Handlers were sometimes allowed to take the dogs home at night, but we weren't supposed to do it too often. It was a complicated situation, because everyone knew that it was important for handlers to bond with their dogs. Cairo spent as much time at my house as he did on the base, and I have no doubt that he was a better working dog because of this. As with any relationship, the more time you spend with someone, the better you know him.

Cairo knew me well. And I knew him.

But the Navy had a responsibility to ensure the safety of its dogs, as well as the safety of people who came into contact with the dogs. Cairo was an amazing dog. He was a reliable and fearsome hunter when so directed, and a playful companion when not at work. But he was probably unusual in that regard. The term "working dog" is deceptive. I was always just as likely to refer to every canine in the program, including Cairo, as an "attack dog." It's not as delicate a description, but it's accurate. And some attack dogs are unpredictable. You can't just take a dog like that and let him roam among civilians. With few exceptions, it's too dangerous.

Cairo was the exception.

I would let Cairo hang out with friends who came to my house to visit. We never had a problem. He seemed to understand instinctively the difference between work and play. Still, I was careful with him. But as time went on, the restrictions around dogs leaving the base were tightened. By the time Cairo returned to active duty, I had already been warned that he'd have to spend almost all his nights at the kennel.

But this was his first day back. I couldn't leave him there.

"Hey, man. I'm taking him home," I said to the Master at Arms in charge of the kennel.

He just smiled. "Yeah, sure."

Cairo seemed strong and healthy. But as we walked through the gates and out into the parking lot, I noticed a slight hitch in his gait. The injury to his right foreleg had healed, but the wound and installation of hardware had left their mark. This didn't mean Cairo would not still be a great working dog, but he would be slightly less agile. As for his battlefield temperament? That remained to be seen. Right now, as he jumped into my truck and curled up against me, he seemed like the same sweet and affectionate dog he'd always been.

"Let's go home, buddy."

That night, I fired up the grill and cooked a couple of big steaks: one for me, one for Cairo. I cut the meat into bite-sized pieces and hand-fed him, so he wouldn't gobble it all at once and make himself sick. Then we sat down on the couch and watched movies together until we both fell asleep.

Sometime after midnight I woke up and turned off the TV. I walked into the bedroom and slid under the covers, with Cairo trailing right behind me.

"Up, boy," I said, gently patting the bed. He didn't need a second invitation. Cairo snuggled up against me all night long. He hogged the bed and gave me a nasty case of night sweats. I didn't mind.

My dog had come home.

CHAPTER 15

By the time we went on our next full deployment, in the fall of 2010, Cairo was ready for active duty.

For the better part of a year we were based in Virginia, training every day for the next extended tour in Afghanistan. There were plenty of training trips where we worked on skydiving, backcountry hiking, or other operations. Cairo accompanied me on almost all those trips. As far as I could tell, there were no psychological scars related to his injury. He wasn't spooked by gunfire or explosions. He didn't seem reluctant to enter a dark building. He obeyed every command he was given.

In other words, he was the same old Cairo. A fantastic dog!

On the next trip to Afghanistan, we were stationed at Jalalabad Air Base. By this time the SEAL canine program was deeply established, so we had a pretty good setup. We had two or three dogs throughout that deployment. As dog handlers, we had our own little hut and training area. We also had a private kennel. This was convenient for the handlers. It was also a bonus for some of the guys who didn't like sharing their living quarters with dogs. Even dogs that were as cool as Cairo!

My friend Angelo was there taking care of his dog, Yari. Angelo was a Master at Arms. He was the kind of guy you trusted with your life on a mission, even though he wasn't a SEAL. We went on tons of operations together, and in addition to being adept at working with dogs, he was a great soldier. We also had another trainer from back home, a former cop named Kevin who took care of a spare dog. Kevin didn't go out on missions with us, but he did valuable work by helping out with the dogs. His experience at "J-Bad" also allowed him to return with knowledge about the kind of work we did in Special Operations. He could then share that information with his bosses and help make adjustments to the canine training program.

We were fortunate on that deployment. We didn't experience any casualties. God knows that wasn't always the case. Just two months before our squadron arrived in Afghanistan, a helicopter crash took the lives of nine American servicemen, including four Navy SEALs.

Our chopper pilots were from the US Army 160th Special Operations Aviation Regiment. Their nickname was "the Night Stalkers." They had ice water in their veins. These guys handled a Black Hawk or a Chinook like they were driving a Maserati. They could weave in and out of the tightest spaces, evade gunfire and RPGs, and set a bird down on the side of a mountain in a dust storm. And they could do it without breaking a sweat. We relied on them to take us to remote areas at the start of a mission, and we relied on them to get us out afterward. They never let us down.

But the risks were great, and we all knew it. No matter how talented and fearless the Night Stalkers might have been, helicopters went down. It was a fact of life. And death.

Being a Navy SEAL is dangerous. That is no secret. But the truth is, you're just as likely to get seriously hurt in a helicopter crash or a training exercise as you are in combat. Every time we went off on a mission, we knew it was possible. We didn't talk about it, but it was always there, in the back of our minds. In fact, the closest I came to serious injury on the

J-Bad deployment was on a mission that involved a helicopter, a dog, and a rope.

The safest and least complicated way to get a dog on the ground during the first stage of a mission (also known as the "mission insert") was to set the helicopter down and jump out. And then hike to the target. Sometimes this wasn't possible. There were occasions when parachuting was the best option, and other times when the pilot would lower the chopper to a safe distance above the insertion site, and the team would exit by fast roping to the ground.

Needless to say, fast roping while holding a seventy-pound dog could be perilous. Cairo was not prone to freaking out about anything. But still . . . you never knew. In some ways, skydiving with a dog, safely packed away in a pouch, barely able to see anything, was less risky than fast roping with a dog.

On this mission, our target was an isolated compound built into the side of a mountain. There was no place to land within several miles of the compound. This meant we would have a two-hour hike after landing. To preserve energy for the mission, we decided to get a little closer and then fast rope out of the chopper.

Ordinarily, when fast roping, I would hook Cairo's har-

Our first trip together. This is Cairo ready for a day of training in Ontario, California.

(Photo by Will Chesney)

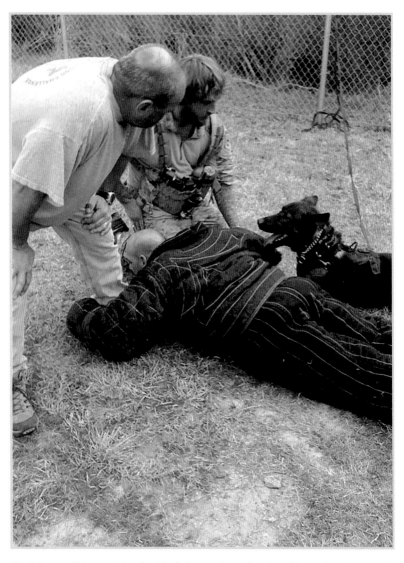

Working on "bite training" with Cairo and another handler and trainer early in my career as a dog handler. Note the bulky bite suit worn by the "target" just inches from Cairo's nose. Cairo was the best—he wouldn't move until instructed to do so.

(Photo from the collection of Will Chesney)

Training in California. This is Cairo in his kennel on the day he broke the door and busted out while I was in a classroom in Ontario. We were both new to the job!

(Photo by Will Chesney)

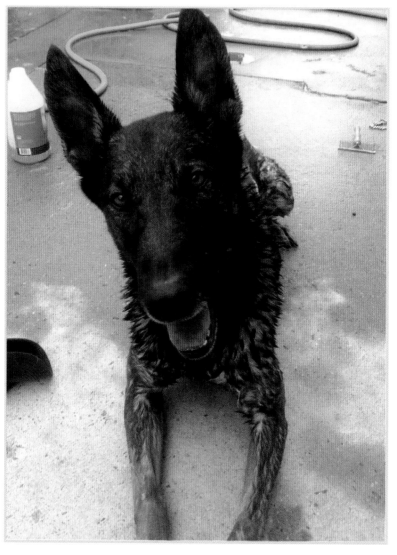

Bath day at the command.   *(Photo by Will Chesney)*

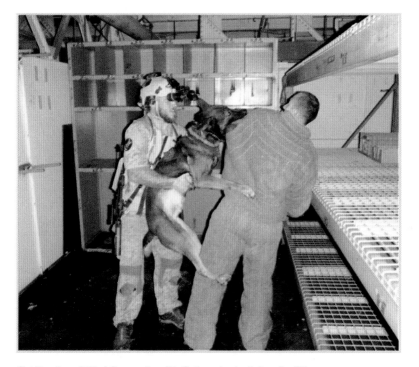

Getting in a little bite work with Cairo at a training facility.

(Photo from the collection of Will Chesney)

Cairo wearing booties and "doggles," and chewing on his favorite ball, shortly before getting seriously wounded on deployment, in the summer of 2009.

(Photo by Will Chesney)

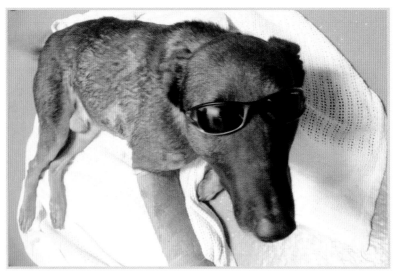

This is Cairo recuperating from gunshot wounds at Bagram, a day after life-saving surgery. He was a tough guy and a quick healer.

(Photo by Will Chesney)

Sitting with Cairo at the vet's office while he recuperated from gunshot wounds. Just trying to help him get comfortable.

(Photo from the collection of Will Chesney)

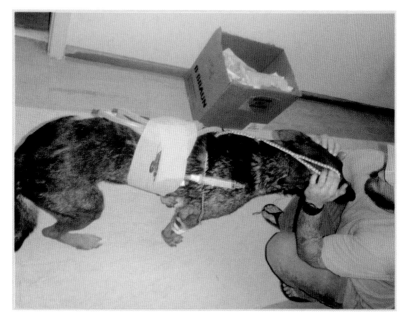

Not long after surgery for his gunshot wounds, Cairo was up and walking around outside. But we had to take frequent breaks.

(Photo by Will Chesney)

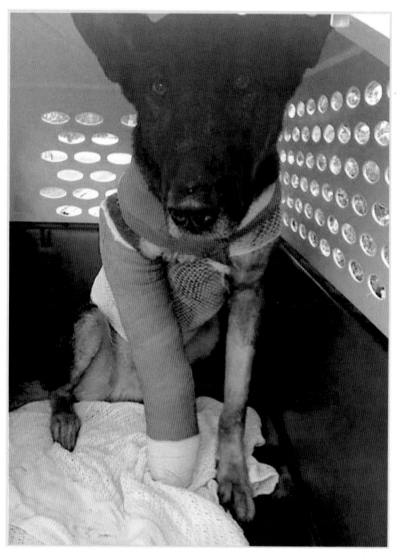

Cairo on his way to Lackland Air Force Base for rehabilitation after getting shot on deployment in Afghanistan.

(Photo by Will Chesney)

Getting in a little training with Cairo at the command in Virginia Beach.

(Photo from the collection of Will Chesney)

This is Cairo hanging out by my desk in the training office at Dam Neck after I became an instructor. The giant bone was a gift from a friend following the Bin Laden raid.

(Photo by Will Chesney)

Cairo with his friends, Sterling and Hagen, after a day at the beach in Virginia.

(Photo by Natalie Kelley)

After so many months of struggle, Cairo finally was retired. This is the day he came to live with Dad.

(Photo by Natalie Kelley)

That's me and Natalie taking Cairo for a ride in the sidecar. Wherever we went, people would naturally stare, but Cairo just loved being out in the open air.

(Photo from the collection of Will Chesney)

A day on the water with Natalie and the dogs. That's Cairo in the middle.

Cairo, right, with his friend Hagen, on the way home from Florida, where Cairo had an unfortunate interaction with a bulldog (note bandages on his left foreleg). Lucky for the bulldog, Cairo did not even respond. He was such a friendly guy!

(Photo by Will Chesney)

ness to my belt and lower us both with my hands on a fixed rope. I also had the option of using something known as a canine fast-rope device.

Fast roping was hard enough without the added weight of a dog. By attaching Cairo to my hip, I was increasing the risk of scorching my hands (despite the heavy gloves) or, worse, losing control and falling. But we did it all the time and never had a problem. Even from a height of fifty or sixty feet, it was a quick trip to the ground, and Cairo always settled down immediately.

This approach to fast roping was my favorite. Once we had feet on the ground, all I had to do was let go and step away with Cairo safely attached to my belt. Then we joined the patrol. The canine fast-rope device was perhaps safer. But it was much slower and more complicated.

It really was an ingenious little tool. But I had rarely used it on missions simply because it took so much extra time and effort. In a traditional fast-rope landing, I just let go and got out of the way, like everyone else. When using the canine fast-rope device, there was one additional step, and it was critical: We had to detach from the device . . . which was attached by a carabiner to the rope . . .

Which was attached to the helicopter.

Picture all of this happening at warp speed. Insertions are designed to be fast. Seconds after the last guy jumps out, the helicopter leaves. The pilot can't just hover fifty feet above the ground for thirty to sixty minutes while we complete our mission. He'd be an easy target for an enemy RPG. Normally this is not a problem. When the last guy hits the ground, he pulls the rope behind him, and the helicopter disappears. But when the last guy out of the chopper is a dog handler using a canine fast-rope device . . . well, that could be a problem.

And on this night, it was.

Cairo and I made a smooth and steady descent. As the ground reached up below us, I figured everything was okay; however, as soon as my boots touched down, I realized that the hillside was very steep. Cairo was uneasy. The rotor wash from the chopper sandblasted us nearly off our feet. Pelted by dust and debris, Cairo recoiled. He began pulling me downhill, away from the spray of the chopper blade.

Normally, this would not have been a big deal. It was a perfectly understandable response on Cairo's part. If I had fast roped with my hands, no problem. Just get away from the rotor wash. Unfortunately, the helicopter was moving uphill.

And we were still attached to the helicopter!

This was one of those occasions when time seemed to stand still. As Cairo tried to drag me downhill while the chopper began pulling us uphill, I knew we were in trouble.

Oh no—we're going to get dragged right off this mountain.

I thought about how it would feel to get yanked into the sky, and perhaps crash into a huge rock along the way. I thought about Cairo dying, and how I'd let him down. I thought about the guys on our squadron, out there in the night, already walking toward the compound. How would they accomplish their mission without a dog to take the heat off them? I was scared and angry and shocked—all at the same time.

And yet, it also seemed kind of funny.

What a way to go. No one is going to believe this.

Had we landed on level ground, without much rotor wash, Cairo would have waited patiently for me to unhook from the device. I could have done this in a matter of seconds. But now, with the rope taut, I was faced with trying to pull myself back up the hill toward the helicopter so that I could gain enough slack to unclip the carabiner. And to do that, I had to convince Cairo to march back into the rotor wash. He did not want to do that, so I scooped him up by the handle on his harness, tossed him a few feet in front of me, and then ran up after him. As soon as I had enough slack, I tried to detach the carabiner in a split second.

No chance.

I did this several times. Each time I tossed him ahead, Cairo would start to run back downhill. I'd have to retrieve him, pick him up again, and march back uphill toward the helicopter. The pilot was in a terrible position. He tried to hold the bird steady until we were released. And with each failed attempt at escape, I was getting more tired.

After what seemed like an eternity, I finally got close enough to make one more attempt at detaching. This one was successful! Instantly, the helicopter peeled off into the night, while I fell to the ground. I was completely exhausted.

And the mission hadn't even started yet!

I rolled over onto my knees and tried to catch my breath. My arms and legs were burning. Cairo walked up and gave me a nudge with his snout, as if to say "Let's go, Dad. Time to work."

I shook my head and stifled a little laugh. It's strange how a potential disaster can seem almost funny.

After it's over.

"What are you looking at?" I said, giving Cairo a pat on the head. "That was your fault."

Not true, really. It was just . . . one of those things. We had the best pilots, the best soldiers, and the best dogs. But sometimes things went wrong. Sometimes things were beyond our control.

"You okay, Cheese?"

The voice coming over the radio was our troop chief. As it turned out, the entire team had been watching me wrestle with the helicopter. Amusement had turned quickly to concern, and then horror, and now relief.

"Yeah, I'll be fine," I said.

"Cairo?"

"He's good, too. Be there in a second."

Thankfully the rest of the night went off without a hitch. We hiked through the mountains to the compound, captured a few bad guys, and we all went home. Safe and sound.

But that was the last time I ever used the fast-rope device.

CHAPTER 16

Saying goodbye was hard, but I tried to think of it as a temporary separation.

This was in early March of 2011, after we returned from Afghanistan. I'd have a few weeks of vacation, but then I'd be reassigned, as would Cairo. This was not unexpected. I'd been a dog handler through two deployments. It was time for me to go back to being an operator. And it was time for Cairo to settle into a less hectic role.

He was close to six years old. He had served his country nobly. He had sustained serious injuries in the line of duty. I felt like he had earned the right to a more peaceful life at home. I figured that home, eventually, would be with me, but I also knew it was too soon for that to happen.

Cairo was a reliable and likable dog. He was still relatively young and fit. It was not surprising that the navy determined that Cairo still had much to offer. He would not be retired. He would become a spare dog.

Instead of being deployed regularly for long periods of time, a spare dog spent most of his days at the kennel in Virginia, or on training exercises. But he was always available for assignments overseas. Spare dogs were usually a bit older. They were low-key and even tempered, which made it easy to assign them to a new handler or unit. They were adaptable, so they could be easily substituted if another dog was wounded or killed.

Selfishly, I hoped Cairo would be retired soon, so that I could take him home. But this wasn't the best idea. Since I was far from retirement age (or health), I'd be traveling all the time. Someone else would have to look after Cairo while I was away. The spare dog assignment was the right way to help Cairo ease into a less stressful life. He would spend more time at home and less time working.

Unfortunately, that time would not be spent with me. I had to give him up. It was part of the job, and I understood it. But it hurt to let him go. Softening the blow was the knowledge that he'd be in good hands. The Master at Arms assigned to him was my good friend Angelo, who knew

Cairo well and was one of the best dog handlers in the navy. It was understood that when Cairo finally did retire, I would have the option to adopt him.

After all, I was still his dad.

Over the course of the next month, I slowly distanced myself from Cairo. I'd stop by and see him once a week or so if he wasn't away on a training exercise. I'd take him for a walk or play with him. But the visits almost made it harder to deal with the separation. When my team was assigned to a training trip in Florida at the end of March, I was eager to get out of town. Being a dog handler is a job that consumes every waking moment. That's why a SEAL typically does only one or two deployments as a handler. He needs a break, and someone else deserves the opportunity.

The Florida trip was like a working vacation. It was a chance to sharpen water skills that might have dulled after multiple deployments to Iraq and Afghanistan, where dry land combat was the norm. Ocean training during the day was followed by relaxed evenings. It was a nice way to unwind after several months in the mountains of Afghanistan. We deserved it.

For two members of our squadron, the trip was cut short after only a few days. There were, suddenly, a pair of openings at the Military Freefall Jumpmaster Course in Arizona. I quickly found myself in Yuma, Arizona, along with Nic Checque, one of my best friends. Like I said earlier, I wasn't the greatest skydiver and didn't really like it all that much, so I would have preferred to stay in South Florida. But getting certified as a free-fall jumpmaster would make me a better SEAL.

Anyway, it wasn't like I had a choice. In the navy, you go where you are told to go. I was told to go to Arizona.

The Jumpmaster course is a rigorous three-week program. Students become better skydivers. They learn how to organize a jump for an entire team. A skydiving insertion is technical and dangerous. Each individual must be highly trained. The exit itself depends on the experience and skill of the pilot, as well as the team member responsible for guiding everyone out of the aircraft. It is a deeply choreographed maneuver. One mistake can be catastrophic for the entire team. Jumpmaster certification, therefore, is a big deal, and I was ready for the challenge.

But someone had other plans.

On the second day of school, I got a phone call from my team leader.

"Pack your gear, Cheese. We need you back in Virginia. Now."

"You've got to be kidding," I said. "I just got here."

"Yeah, I know. Something came up. I can't tell you anything else. Just get home."

After nine years in the navy, I knew better than to pump him for more info. Stuff happens. Plans change. You get an order, you follow it. Then you follow another one. In due time, more would be revealed. Hopefully, this would be something interesting.

"Okay," I said. "I'll leave tonight."

There was a pause.

"Hey, Cheese. One other thing."

"What's that?"

"Pick up Cairo when you get here."

I smiled and nodded to myself.

"Got it."

In a Jumpmaster class of two dozen students, Nic and I were the only SEALs. When he asked why I had been recalled to Virginia, I told him, "I have no idea. Guess I'll find out soon enough."

It was perplexing. I couldn't figure out why I had been recalled and Nic hadn't. I can say without hesitation that Nic was a better operator than I was. The only logical explanation was that, for some reason, Cairo was needed. And I had been Cairo's handler for a long time.

We were a package deal.

CHAPTER 17

I flew overnight and arrived in Virginia the next morning. I drove straight to the kennel to pick up Cairo. I still had no clue as to why I had been recalled, or why I had been reassigned to the role of dog handler—after only about a month away from the job.

Nor did I care. You didn't have to be a genius to figure out that something unique was about to happen. This obviously was a mission that required the services of a reliable working dog, and Cairo was about as reliable as they come. I was lucky enough to be his handler.

It was hard to know why certain SEALs were picked for certain assignments, particularly when there was very little advance notice. Sometimes guys were unavailable. They had the right to turn down an assignment if it conflicted with a serious personal matter or another professional obligation. Married men with kids and other responsibilities were more likely to take a pass. That was okay. They'd earned the privilege, and everyone understood when it happened (although it didn't happen that often). I was still young and single. Being a SEAL was my life. If this was a plum assignment, I wanted in. And the fact that I would get to work again with Cairo made it even more appealing.

When I met him at the kennel that morning, Cairo bounced around like a puppy. I let him stand and put his paws on my chest. I gave him a big hug and hooked him up to a lead.

"Time to go to work, pal."

Information came out in a trickle. I was used to being told only what I needed to know, when I needed to know it. This was different. From the moment I was instructed to return from Jumpmaster School, I sensed an unusual level of secrecy. This continued when our squadron gathered in the Team Room for the first official briefing.

There were two dozen of us in the room when the master chief began his briefing. He told us we were going to be part of an important and secret mission. He didn't say where the mission would take place. He didn't tell us the objective of the mission or the reason behind it. He did say that our destination was some sort of terrorist operation that resembled the compounds we had all encountered in Afghanistan. He also said the mission would be challenging and dangerous. Beyond that, he had nothing specific to offer.

"You'll know more at the appropriate time," he said.

He then told us that the members of the squadron selected for this assignment would be divided into four teams. Cairo and I were assigned to Team 4, which would handle perimeter duties associated with the target. The first three teams would be assault teams. The person in charge of Team 4 was Rob O'Neill, a good friend of mine and one of the men I admired most in the squadron. Rob was nearly a decade older than me. He had a ton of experience in high-profile deployments all over the world. I had enormous faith in him as a leader.

Even though I didn't know the details of the mission, I had a feeling that it was something special. I was excited to be a part of it. I had a few moments like this during my SEAL career—times when I felt lucky to be working alongside guys like Rob and Nic . . . and many others who will remain nameless.

I'm not trying to be falsely humble. I took part in a lot of important missions, and I'm proud of the things I accomplished. I came from a little town in Texas and made it all the way through the funnel and wound up on the most elite SEAL team. It was a dream come true. But I know that my accomplishments pale in comparison to many of the men with whom I served. That's one of the things about being a SEAL. All you have to do is look at some of your teammates, and you'll realize how much you still have to learn.

For the better part of a week, we hung out in Virginia, discussing the mission in vague terms. There was a target within a compound somewhere. Our assignment was to remove or eliminate the target.

Where?

When?

We didn't know.

On Sunday, April 10, we packed our gear and drove to a training facility in North Carolina. We didn't know what to expect when we got there. But when you have a week to discuss a mission shrouded in secrecy, there will be speculation. It's probably not surprising to know that the name of Osama bin Laden came up several times during that week. Bin Laden was the leader of the terrorist organization known as Al Qaeda. He had ordered the attacks of September 11, 2001. And ever since that time, he had been hunted by the US military.

Maybe, we thought, this is it. Maybe we're finally going after bin Laden.

For us, and for the entire US military, bin Laden was the most wanted criminal in the world. Take down bin Laden, and we'd put a deep and lasting gash into his terrorist organization. It wouldn't end the war. We all knew that. But his capture or death would at least be a measure of revenge for the deaths of nearly three thousand civilians who perished on 9/11. That was worth something. For almost a decade, bin Laden had eluded capture, and we all wanted to take him down.

When you serve in Special Operations, you can't get caught up in a single-minded pursuit. Every day brings a new mission, a new objective. You treat each with professionalism and clarity, and then you move on. Regardless of what the objective of this mission might be, we would treat it no differently.

And yet . . .

Oh, how I hoped the rumors were true.

I was excited as I made the ninety-minute drive with Cairo to North Carolina. We were briefed by our commanding officer, Captain Perry "Pete" Van Hooser. In addition to the two dozen members of our squadron, there were several people in attendance whom I did not recognize. Some were navy officers. Others were US intelligence officials. I'd sat through hundreds of mission briefings in my career, but this one felt different. It didn't take long to figure out why that was the case.

Captain Pete thanked us for our time, and then revealed the true nature of our mission.

"We're going after UBL," he said.

"UBL" referred to Usama bin Laden. While he was commonly referred to as "Osama" in Western media, intelligence agencies such as the Central Intelligence Agency (CIA) and Federal Bureau of Investigation (FBI) preferred a different spelling: *Usama*. It was just a different way of translating his name from Arabic. Didn't matter to me. At the very sound of those initials, the hair on the back of my neck stood up. I revealed no emotion; nor did anyone else in the room. The mood was sober, professional.

The briefing went on for several hours. Years of intelligence work had apparently pinpointed bin Laden's position. He was living in a large housing compound in Abbottabad, a city in eastern Pakistan. This was not shocking. The war against terrorism had been staged mostly in Iraq and Afghanistan. But it had long been thought that bin Laden might be hiding somewhere else, in a country sympathetic to the Al Qaeda mission. Pakistan was a logical answer.

It was surprising to learn that bin Laden was not barricaded in an underground bunker or cave somewhere in the mountains, but rather hiding in plain sight! He took daily walks in a flowing white robe. He circled the compound for hours at a time. This routine earned him the nickname "the Pacer."

There was no guarantee that the Pacer was in fact bin Laden, but the intelligence officials at the briefing seemed confident. He was well over six feet tall and lean, with a long gray beard. He looked very much like bin Laden. He behaved in the manner of someone important, never taking part in the work of others. And the compound sprawled like nothing else in the neighborhood. There were walls ranging from roughly ten to twenty feet in height. The compound included a large three-story house, a guesthouse, and other smaller structures that were likely used for housing animals.

The preparation that went into this briefing was impressive, to say the least. This was an example of what could be accomplished through a combination of advanced technology and dogged determination. Here, right in front of us, were high-resolution photographs of Osama bin Laden's home!

We knew where he was. All we had to do now was remove him.

As the briefing progressed, we were told of other options that had been discussed and discarded. The "softest" approach would have been to ask the Pakistani government to either hand over bin Laden or join US forces on a mission. Pakistan was considered sympathetic to Al Qaeda, so this seemed like a terrible idea. An air strike might have been effective, but also would have been devastating. The explosive power required to guarantee success was so great that it would have leveled the entire neighborhood, if not most of the city of Abbottabad.

Many innocent people would have been killed.

The only answer was a surgical strike led by a Special

Operations unit. We would breach the compound and extract UBL—dead or alive. It was a dangerous mission, with a significant likelihood of casualties on the American side. It also was the mission of a lifetime. I couldn't believe we were getting this opportunity!

My enthusiasm did not wane, even as the risks were laid out in graphic fashion: one of our helicopters being shot down by RPGs; heavy resistance within the compound; the high probability that the entire place was rigged with explosives and that we'd all be blown to bits. That was fine with me. I mean, no one wants to get shot or killed. But as long as we got bin Laden, I was okay with anything else that might happen.

One of my first thoughts while listening to the briefing was, "Well, guess I won't be coming home from this one."

My second thought was, "But as long as we get this guy, I'm good with it."

CHAPTER 18

The mission was given the name Operation Neptune Spear. The reason this name had been chosen was because Neptune's spear is a trident, and a trident is part of the US Naval Special Warfare insignia. A trident is a three-pronged spear. Each prong of the trident represents a portion of the operational capacity of the SEALs: sea, air, land.

So, Operation Neptune Spear it was.

Made sense to me.

We spent most of the next week in North Carolina, training from sunup until deep into the night. We physically rehearsed the entire mission, over and over, using a full-sized model of the compound.

When I first saw this thing, I was blown away. Video and photos are helpful. But there's nothing quite like practicing an operation on a full-scale replica of the target. It was reassuring to know that everyone understood the magnitude of this mission. They would spare no expense in providing us with everything we needed to do the job right.

It should be noted that the model allowed us to train on exterior tactics only. We didn't know the interior layout of the buildings. But that was okay. We knew from experience that a floor plan was as likely to mess you up as it was to help. Even the best satellite or drone photos would not provide a foolproof interior layout. The best you could do was guess. If you studied and memorized a floor plan, and then found something different when you got inside, it could compromise the mission. Better to just go with the flow.

In some ways, every mission was like playing pickup basketball with a group of guys you know well. Read and react: "You go this way, I'll go that way." There was always a basic outline for the mission. But we also had the freedom to make changes based on the circumstances we encountered. There was more intelligence than usual on this one, but I had no doubt that once we were on the ground, something unexpected would happen.

Cairo was deeply involved in most of the rehearsals and performed like the pro he was—with one notable exception. And, again, this was my fault.

We were rehearsing a breach of one of the compound gates, using live explosives to blow the door open. Since Cairo wasn't needed for the breach, I had left him in the parking lot, in the back seat of a navy-issued Chevy Suburban. When I say "back seat," I mean loose in the vehicle. I had gotten used to doing this with Cairo over the years. If I went somewhere and left him in the car for a few minutes, I'd rarely bother putting him in his kennel. He could be trusted to chill out in the car until I returned.

We used to call him "Houdini," a nickname earned after multiple escapes. This is going to sound like fiction, but I swear it's true. Cairo learned how to squeeze his foreleg through the front grate and use his paw to lift the latch on the kennel. If for some reason that didn't work, he would use his teeth and his legs to twist the front grate, until eventually he created enough of a gap to squeeze through.

Sometimes it was easier to just let him lie down on the back seat of the car. He was happier.

Anyway, on this particular night, Cairo was loose in the Suburban when the breaching and explosions began. I didn't think anything of it until we were through with the exercise and got back to the SUV. Inside, Cairo was bouncing around, panting and whining. He was also covered with tufts of white fabric that made it look like he'd been out in a snowstorm. In fact, he'd been creating a storm of a different type in the car. He had ripped the padded headrests off their foundations and shredded them to bits.

"Cairo!" I yelled as I opened the door.

He jumped into my arms and then fell to the ground. He began running around like crazy. I quickly got him leashed up and took him for a short walk. (At least he hadn't gone to the bathroom in the car!) I wasn't really mad at Cairo. He was my responsibility, after all, and I had left him unattended. I should have known better.

"You know not to do that again, right?" my team leader said to me.

I did, of course. Leaving Cairo in the car, unattended, while explosives rocked the surrounding area, was unfair. I do not think he was frightened by the blasts. In fact, I'm pretty sure he was just excited. To Cairo, explosions and gunfire were a signal to begin work. To seek out a bad guy and engage. I can only imagine how confusing it would have been for him to hear those blasts and not be able to do anything about it.

After that, I crated him during any training exercise in which he was not an active participant.

Better safe than sorry.

We left North Carolina the following weekend and traveled straight to another training facility in the Southwest. This site was designed to mimic not just the mission but the geography and climate in which it would take place. We trained at altitude, in the desert. Over and over we boarded helicopters, flew a distance approximate to that of flying from Jalalabad to Abbottabad, and fast roped out of helicopters. Cairo made every exit with me.

By the end of the week, we had the insertion down cold. In all honesty, it was not that complicated. What made this unique, and uniquely lethal, was that we were going after the most high-profile target in SEAL history. If we screwed up, the fallout would be felt for years.

And we'd probably all be killed.

By the end of April, we had it down cold. We had rehearsed the mission dozens of times. We knew it by heart.

Two Black Hawk helicopters would travel under cover of darkness from J-Bad to Abbottabad. My chopper included guys from two teams: one for perimeter security and the other an assault team. The chopper would land outside the compound and drop off the perimeter team first. That included me, Cairo, Rob, an interpreter, a couple of snipers, and a gunner. Then our helicopter would hover over the main house, allowing the assault team to fast rope to the roof. Eventually the plan was modified slightly, with Rob joining the rooftop team to give us one more shooter on the main house.

My job was to help hold security outside the compound, perhaps against Al Qaeda forces, local law enforcement, or curious locals wondering what was going on in their neighborhood. We didn't know whether the locals knew that bin Laden was in their midst, but it was certainly possible. We had to protect the perimeter of the compound so that the assault teams could do their work inside.

If the initial assault turned up nothing, or if bin Laden was missing, I would bring Cairo inside to do a more intensive search. It seemed reasonable that the Al Qaeda leader would have more than a few hiding places within the compound.

Meanwhile, the other helicopter would hover over the courtyard—within or just above the compound walls, at a spot somewhere between the main house and the guesthouse. From there, assault team members would fast rope out of the helicopter while snipers provided security from the chopper. This helicopter faced the most dangerous task. It would be open to attack for as long as it took the assault team to exit.

If this sounds complicated and dangerous . . . well, yes, it was. But no more so than any number of missions we had successfully completed in the past. We had the advantage in terms of training, technology, intelligence, and weaponry. We had experience and the element of surprise (or, at least, we hoped we did). But there were things we didn't know, and those were the variables that pushed the mission into uncharted territory.

It was possible that the most wanted terrorist in history would have a heavily armed security force. Also, there was a long history of terrorists going out with a bang when cornered. We expected to encounter suicide bombers within the compound. Finally, there was the possibility of interference from the Pakistani police or military. They would not like the idea of a US military force flying within its borders. They could accuse us of attacking their country.

We were well prepared, but there were things that could go wrong. Things beyond our control.

At the end of April, we received word that United States President Barack Obama was likely to approve the mission. I felt confident and proud.

When desert training ended and we all returned to Virginia, we were instructed to get our affairs in order. For me, that meant making sure that my life insurance premiums were paid and that I had a will on record somewhere. Not that I had much to leave behind. I'm sure those last few days in April were particularly tough on the married guys. They had to say goodbye to their wives and kids without being able to tell them why they seemed a little sadder than usual.

I did not call my mother before leaving. That was standard practice for me. For one thing, my mom did not hear very well, so phone calls were a challenge. Also, she worried too much as it was. If I had called her this time, she would have suspected something. So I just sent her a quick text and kept it short and simple.

I did call my father. That, too, was standard practice when I left on deployment. But this time felt different. Even though I'd been on my own for a long time and moved across the country, I still felt close to my dad. I wanted to say goodbye . . . just in case.

It wasn't a long conversation. I told him I was deploying unexpectedly. There was something important going on, and I was part of it. I also told him I might not make it back. He knew better than to ask for specifics.

"Be careful, okay?" he said.

"I will," I replied. "And Dad?"

"Yes, boy?"

"I love you."

There was a long pause before he responded. I can only imagine what he was thinking.

"I love you, too."

CHAPTER 19

In the back of a specially adapted MH-60 Black Hawk heli-copter, I closed my eyes and let the music wash over me. Everyone had a routine on a mission. Some guys slept on the way to an operation. Others tried to talk, although this was challenging given the noise in the aircraft. Some guys said nothing and merely rehearsed the mission in their heads.

Through a small iPod strapped to my shoulder, I listened to music: loud heavy rock or country. As the music screeched into my earbuds, I leaned over and gave Cairo a pat on the head.

The Black Hawk is much smaller and quicker than a Chinook, so we were packed pretty tight. Cairo and I were both on the floor. He sat between my legs, calm as always. I hooked a thumb through his harness and rubbed his back. He was wearing the same bloodstained vest he'd worn on every mission since getting shot the previous year. He arched his head and looked up at me eagerly.

A dozen of us sat in the back of the chopper, along with a couple of Night Stalkers up front. Rob sat next to me on the flight. He was smart. He remembered to bring a folding director's chair! We looked at each other a couple of times but didn't say anything.

Approximately ninety minutes earlier, around 11:00 P.M. on the night of May 2, 2011, we had left J-Bad in two MH-60s. Now we were in Pakistani airspace and closing in on the city of Abbottabad. A voice crackled over the radio to let us know we were ten minutes out. This was standard operating procedure, but like so many other things about Operation Neptune Spear, it didn't *feel* standard.

I turned off my music and envisioned the insertion for roughly the hundredth time. I checked my radio, my weapon, my night vision goggles. I took a quick glance at the laminated card we each had been given. On it was a map of the compound. I made sure Cairo was ready to go.

"Three minutes!"

The two helicopters had flown in tandem to this point. As

we approached the compound, the other chopper veered off toward the compound walls. I lost sight of it.

"Thirty seconds!"

We made our approach to an area just outside the compound. The pilot set the Black Hawk down expertly, right on the "X" (the precise spot where we were supposed to land). I jumped out with Cairo, the snipers, and the interpreter. We immediately began working the perimeter. I looked back over my shoulder and noticed the Black Hawk still on the ground. Seconds later, the rest of the team disembarked. I had no idea what was happening, but it certainly didn't look good.

Uh-oh . . . we just landed and already something has gone wrong.

Plans can change in a heartbeat. It can happen on any mission. For some reason the assault team on our Black Hawk had redirected. Instead of fast roping to the roof of the main house, inside the compound, they had decided to leave the helicopter now and breach from the outside wall. But my job remained unchanged.

I took Cairo off leash and began working him in a clockwise direction around the outside of the compound. Explosives went off behind me. This was the unmistakable sound of breachers at work. They were blowing up doors and gates to enter the compound. I walked alongside Cairo as he put his nose to the ground in a thorough search for explosives.

As we rounded a corner, I looked up at the compound wall. In the distance, I could see something sticking up, almost resting on the top of the wall. It was the tail of a helicopter. But only the tail. The rest of the aircraft, I figured, must have been on the other side. It didn't look like a crash, but more like a landing that hadn't quite worked. It seemed so strange that my first thought was:

Hey, that helicopter looks just like one of ours!

There was a reason for the similarity: It *was* one of ours!

What I did not know at the time was that the first Black Hawk had run into trouble while hovering inside the walls of the compound. As the helicopter tried to maintain a steady hover, the team members prepared to fast rope down. But the chopper began to shake violently. A combination of hot, dry air and the solid walls of the compound had caused the chopper to get caught in its own rotor wash.

Why hadn't this happened during any of our training exercises? Well, because our model of the compound was surrounded by walls that were not made of solid material. This allowed wind, including air whipped up by the rotor of a helicopter, to pass harmlessly through. In Abbottabad, the compound's solid walls created very different conditions for the helicopter. It was like being sucked into a whirlpool.

Fortunately, the pilot recognized what was happening. Rather than fight the vortex, he orchestrated a perfectly executed "controlled crash." He turned the nose of the Black Hawk away from the walls and dropped it into the ground as gently as possible, leaving the tail on top of one of the walls. No one was hurt. Everyone jumped out without a scratch, and the mission went on as planned.

The pilot of our chopper had witnessed the entire event from the cockpit. That's why he had decided not to elevate after dropping off me and Cairo and the rest of the security team. Instead, he told the assaulters that they would be unable to hover inside the compound. They had to exit the craft now.

All of this happened within a matter of minutes. It had no impact on the operation. My teammates blasted open gates and doors to get into the compound. I used Cairo to search for explosives or insurgents hiding out beyond the compound walls.

After two complete laps, it was determined that the perimeter was secure. I was astonished. If this really was the home of Osama bin Laden, how could there not be explosives rimming the compound? Where were the bombs and snipers?

It was almost too easy.

With several of our team holding security outside the compound, I began to work my way inside. By the time I got to the main house, only ten to fifteen minutes after we had landed, the place was a mess. It was littered with debris and bodies. I was relieved to see that none of my teammates were among the casualties.

The floor was covered with broken glass. I repeatedly scooped up Cairo and carried him over the shards before setting him down to inspect another room. We methodically worked our way through the first floor. By now there were more than twenty SEALs inside the compound. Most were in the main house.

Although gunfire seemed to have stopped, it was still a dangerous situation. For all I knew, a dozen bad guys were hiding in the basement, or behind false walls, or almost anywhere. Trip wires connected to bombs could be hanging from the ceiling or doorways. We couldn't let our guard down for a second. More than once we had reached what we thought was the completion of an operation, only to be surprised by a gun-toting insurgent leaping out from a hiding place.

We had lost more than a few people that way, so we never relaxed until we were back on the base.

The mission wasn't over . . . until it was over.

With Cairo by my side, I made my way to the second floor, trailing behind a growing train of operators. I would guide Cairo wherever he was needed, as instructed. I tried to keep his attention focused on explosive odor. It seemed impossible that the place hadn't been rigged with bombs. Our best hope was that Cairo could sniff out the danger before it had a chance to hurt us. That's why I took him room to room on the first two floors. Even though we seemed to have gained control of the structure, I wanted to be sure that there were no surprises. Using Cairo's amazing nose was the best way to do that.

As I climbed the stairs to the third floor, things got busier. We had a bunch of men on the third floor, but there was no fighting. I heard a lot of talking. One of my teammates came down the stairs while I was walking up.

"It's crazy up there, Cheese," he said. "You can go up if you want, but I don't think they need the dog. It's over."

It's over . . .

That could only mean one thing: Osama bin Laden was in the house. And now he was either dead or captured. I wanted to go upstairs, to see for myself what was happening. But I wasn't going to disregard a teammate's suggestion just to satisfy my own curiosity. I trusted my teammates. If one of them said that Cairo wasn't needed, then Cairo wasn't needed. His word was good enough for me.

As I walked into a second-floor hallway, Rob came down the stairs from the third floor. We both walked into another room. Our eyes met. He nodded and smiled. It was a look I had rarely seen from Rob, who was typically all business during an operation.

"Dude," he said. "I think I just shot him."

"What?" I said. "Seriously?"

Rob nodded. "Yeah."

He didn't use bin Laden's name, but I knew exactly who he meant. We both froze for a few seconds in the hallway. This information had already been conveyed to our ground force commander. Moments later, his voice came over the radio, as he passed the information on to Admiral William McRaven, the SEAL in charge of Joint Special Operations Command.

"For God and country, Geronimo, Geronimo, Geronimo, EKIA."

We had a bunch of code words used to signify parts of Operation Neptune Spear. "Geronimo" referred to Osama bin Laden. The second half of the message, "EKIA," represented the outcome of that confrontation: "Enemy Killed in Action."

"Yeah!" I said, holding my hand high for Rob to smack. And right there, on the second floor of Osama bin Laden's house, we shared a high five.

Let me explain something. I had never high-fived anyone before, during or after a mission. I had never seen any of my teammates celebrate in this manner. It was uncool, unprofessional, unacceptable. This was not a game. We were not cowboys. We were not vigilantes. We were part of an elite special operations unit that took pride in doing its job with professionalism and efficiency.

We got in, we got out, we moved on to the next assignment.

A high five?

Come on, man. Who does that?

Well, on May 2, 2011, I did it. And it absolutely felt like the correct response at the time. It was pure, unbridled joy.

The mission did not end with the announcement of bin Laden's death. As my teammates gathered files, flash drives, laptop computers, and other material from the third floor, Cairo and I continued to search for explosives. We slowly made our way outside into the courtyard, and finally back out to the perimeter. I could see several small groups of people approaching the compound from the surrounding neighborhood. Not a huge mob, but enough to be of concern. This was a big city, and it wouldn't take long for us to be outnumbered by the locals.

Having Cairo out there was a big help. A large and imposing attack dog will sometimes do more to discourage curiosity seekers than a handful of armed soldiers.

A couple of members of the team rigged the downed helicopter with timed charges so that we could blow it up. We couldn't leave a piece of equipment behind after a mission, especially one as valuable as a Black Hawk helicopter. Photos and video of a downed US helicopter screamed "failure" to the world. The chopper was also loaded with equipment and weaponry. We couldn't let that stuff fall into the wrong hands.

Four huge MH-47 Chinook helicopters—"flying school buses," we used to call them—had taken off from Jalalabad shortly after we left. Two of the buses were loaded with a Quick Reaction Force (QRF) comprised of a couple dozen SEALs. They had waited at the border, ready to jump in if disaster struck. The other Chinooks had crossed into Pakistani airspace and landed in a remote area, where they could be summoned if needed for help during extraction.

We needed that help now.

The first Black Hawk was already on its way back to Abbottabad when we called in the Chinooks. A few members of the team went back to J-Bad in the Black Hawk, along with bin Laden's body. The rest of us waited for one of the Chinooks in a grassy area just outside the compound.

As bad luck would have it, the Chinook drew near just as the explosive charge on the rigged Black Hawk was about to blow. We were counting it down when the Chinook came into view.

"Thirty seconds!"

There was an anxious moment when we realized that the Chinook was going to fly over the compound at almost the exact moment that the Black Hawk would explode. And yet, our team leader remained calm.

"Abort," he said into the radio. "Do a racetrack."

This was the team leader's way of letting the pilot know that something was wrong and that he needed to take a lap overhead (a "racetrack") before landing.

"Copy that," came the reply.

As the Black Hawk exploded and burst into flames, the Chinook completed a wide circle over the compound. It flew dramatically through a giant mushroom cloud of smoke before settling into a safe landing nearby. The whole thing looked like something out of a movie.

We climbed aboard and huddled together as the Chinook lifted into the air and pulled away. I looked out the window and could see the flames and smoke rising above the compound. Cairo was at my feet, sitting calmly, but I reached down and scooped him up so that he could sit on my lap.

It was hard to hear much of anything over the roar of the Chinook. That was okay, because I didn't really feel like talking. Neither did anyone else. I think we all were in a bit of shock.

I pulled out my iPod and began scrolling through my music. I stopped on one of my favorite songs by the country singer Travis Tritt. The name of the song was "It's a Great Day to Be Alive." With Cairo settling into me, and my brothers all around me, I leaned back and closed my eyes . . . and sang along in my head.

CHAPTER 20

The flight back to Jalalabad was in some ways the most dangerous part of the mission. We were in hostile airspace, lumbering along in a giant flying school bus. We were an easy and overmatched target for a Pakistani fighter jet. But I don't remember feeling worried. I hadn't expected to return from Operation Neptune Spear, and now that safety was within reach . . . well, it was a little hard to comprehend.

We landed first at J-Bad, around three o'clock in the morning. Admiral McRaven was there to greet us, along with some other Navy brass and intelligence experts from the CIA and FBI. They pored over the materials we had brought back and conducted interviews with just about everyone involved in the raid. I knew from experience that it could take days or weeks to construct an accurate picture of what happened on a mission.

But this was Osama bin Laden. The world would want to know what happened. Right away.

The next stop was Bagram. We all hung out together in an airplane hangar, eating a massive breakfast, telling jokes, and celebrating the biggest operation of our lives. A large-screen TV had been brought into the building so that we could watch as the event was reported back in the States.

At 11:35 in the evening, local time, President Obama walked to a podium in the White House and addressed the world.

"Good evening. Tonight, I can report to the American people and to the world that the United States has conducted an operation that killed Osama bin Laden, the leader of Al Qaeda, and a terrorist who's responsible for the murder of thousands of innocent men, women, and children . . .

"A small team of Americans carried out the operation with extraordinary courage and capability. No Americans were harmed. They took care to avoid civilian casualties. After a firefight, they killed Osama bin Laden and took custody of his body."

On a night filled with extraordinary events, this was

perhaps the strangest: to be sitting in an airplane hangar at Bagram, eating breakfast, watching the president of the United States announce to the world the outcome of a top secret mission. And it all was happening just a couple of hours after we had completed that mission.

I took a bite out of a sandwich and looked at the TV screen. I looked around the room, at the greatest group of guys I'd ever get to work with. And then I looked to my left. There, less than twenty feet away, was the body of Osama bin Laden.

What an incredible night.

Within thirty-six hours we were back in Virginia. We were treated like heroes. Robert Gates, the US secretary of defense, paid a visit. Everyone on the mission was awarded the Silver Star for "gallantry in action against an enemy of the United States." It was a disappointment to me that Cairo did not receive a Silver Star. He was just as important a part of the mission as anyone else. He risked just as much.

But at least he wasn't overlooked entirely. A few days later, the team went to Fort Campbell, Kentucky, where the 160th Airborne is based. There, we met with President Obama and Vice President Joe Biden. The president delivered a short speech. It was a chance for him to "say on behalf of all Americans and people around the globe, job well done." He seemed emotional and proud.

We were presented with a Presidential Unit Citation. In return, we gave the president a framed American flag that had been with us on the mission. The front of the frame was inscribed with the words, "From the Joint Task Force Operation Neptune's Spear, 01 May 2011: 'For God and country. Geronimo.'"

Before the talk, the president had been briefed by our commander about some of the details of the mission, including the fact that Cairo had been an important member of the team. Obama's reaction?

"I want to meet this dog."

Someone jokingly advised the president that if he wanted to say hello to Cairo, it might be wise to bring some treats. He was, after all, an attack dog. Both the president and vice president walked into a separate room where I was waiting with Cairo.

"So, this is the famous Cairo," President Obama said.

"Yes, sir," I replied.

Obama nodded. He said some nice things about Cairo

and me and everyone on the team. We shook hands and took some pictures. Both the president and vice president gave Cairo a gentle little pat on the back. Good dog that he was, he didn't even flinch. He seemed to be having a good time.

Of course, Cairo was wearing his muzzle the entire time. I wasn't about to take a chance in a situation like that. Can you imagine if Cairo took a nip at the president? Now that would have been a lousy footnote to the biggest mission in SEAL history: me standing next to the president of the United States, asking, "Am I fired?"

CHAPTER 21

When I returned to Afghanistan for my next deployment, in the spring of 2012, dogs remained a big part of my working life. Unfortunately, none of those dogs was Cairo.

I was assigned to a team that was responsible for training new members of the Afghan special forces. The assignment would last a couple of months.

I didn't have a lot of respect for the Afghan military. Their fighters didn't like to fight, and their training was substandard. There were exceptions, but I think most US soldiers felt that the Afghan military was not much help. But the long-term goal was for the country to wage its own battles. That wasn't going to happen without a lot of support from the United States military. This is where I came in. I was part of a group of instructors that also included another SEAL, a handful of Army Rangers, some guys from Delta Force (which is an elite special operations army unit), and a few private contractors. I don't know if any of us were happy to be there, but it was an important job.

The time went by quickly. Pretty soon I rejoined my squadron at Forward Operating Base Shank, located in Logar Province in eastern Afghanistan. It felt good to be back with my teammates, doing the kind of work I had been trained to do. If there was any letdown following Operation Neptune Spear, I didn't notice it. An important bad guy had been eliminated, but the war against terrorism continued.

My job had changed. I was no longer a dog handler. I was strictly an operator. To be honest, I enjoyed the freedom that came with my new role. That doesn't mean I didn't miss Cairo. I certainly did. But I was lucky. If I needed a "Cairo fix," I didn't have to go far. He'd been deployed to Logar, as well, to be utilized as a spare dog on-site. He was available for duty on a moment's notice. I stopped by to see him and Angelo once a week or so, and Cairo was always affectionate and playful. I do think he missed me. But we each had a job to do, and for now those jobs did not overlap.

In mid-June, we got word of a high-value target hiding out in a desert compound. Nothing strange about that. It was a mission that in many ways was no different from a hundred others. Same afternoon briefing, same nighttime helicopter ride, same landing in the middle of nowhere, same hike to the target.

Including support personnel, we had close to thirty people out there in the desert. There was an unusual amount of radio chatter that night, including a conversation indicating the enemy knew we were coming. Now, sometimes they would say this kind of stuff as a trick. They wanted to make us think they were prepared, when that wasn't really the case. It didn't matter. We weren't going to call off a mission just because the enemy knew we were coming. We might make some changes, but it wasn't about to scare us off.

We hiked for a couple of miles before the compound came into view. It was small—just two modest buildings, each two stories in height. Pretty much a standard Afghan desert setup. We followed a rough, barely visible path to a distance of one hundred meters from the compound. My team took cover in a shallow ditch while waiting for orders. As always, we were patient, careful.

After a few minutes, the team leader ordered me and another guy, Tommy, toward the second building.

"Cheese, I want you guys on the roof to hold security. Okay?"

"Got it."

We rushed to the building and held our positions. Then we began creeping slowly along its length. Suddenly, shots rang out from above us. The crackle of automatic gunfire.

Pop-pop-pop!

I couldn't look up, but I knew the gunfire was probably coming from a second-story window. Someone had seen us approaching. Tommy, who was a few feet away from me and had a better angle, returned fire. I held tight to the outside wall so that I wouldn't throw him off in any way. As soon as he stopped firing, I sprinted back and out into the surrounding terrain to get a better look.

Soon enough, another operator, Curt, joined me, along with an explosives ordinance disposal (EOD) specialist named Richard. (EODs are the "bomb squad." They are called in to help dispose of or detonate explosive devices before they can harm anyone.)

The three of us stayed there for a minute. We were fanned out in a row, with ten or fifteen feet separating each of us. I kept my rifle trained on the window, just waiting for someone to pop up.

"Come on . . . show yourself."

The next thing I heard was the sound of breaking glass. It sounded like someone had thrown a rock through a window. I knew instantly what it meant. A thought ran through my head just before everything went dark.

Grenade . . .

I don't know how much time passed—probably no more than ten or fifteen seconds. There was a crushing pain in my lower back, as if someone had walloped me with a baseball bat. Then there was a loss of awareness.

Next thing I knew, I was on my knees, holding my rifle. I looked up at the window but saw nothing. As I started to move, I felt a blistering pain in my lower back. And I could hear Richard moaning. He'd been blown several meters away, and his uniform had been badly charred. I looked around and saw Curt, who appeared to be uninjured, but I couldn't tell for sure.

In my memory, I stood up and fired my rifle at the same window through which the grenade had passed. But memory is an unreliable thing when you've just been blown up. As I watched the drone surveillance video a few days later, I saw a guy rocked by a grenade. I was standing, but not responding. My gun remained low and at my side. I did not fire a shot.

The scene was chaotic after the blast. We quickly had men all around the compound and on the roof of the building. I could hear shots being fired as I lurched out into the field. I remember thinking, *You're kind of unprotected here, dude. What are you doing?*

Good question. No answer.

I made my way toward some guys who were holding security on the perimeter.

"You okay, Cheese?" one of them asked.

"Uh . . . not sure. I think I got hit."

A corpsman arrived on the scene. (A corpsman is the navy's version of a medic.) He told me to be still and began looking for wounds. This guy was awesome. His name was Anthony. He was a SEAL who hadn't gone through Green Team but talked of it all the time.

Anthony was an amazing corpsman. He was incredibly calm and focused under pressure. When you get wounded in battle, there is an overwhelming sense of confusion, not to mention pain. I had no idea what was wrong with me, and I wasn't sure I wanted to know.

"Drop your pants!" Anthony instructed.

"Huh?"

He pushed me to the ground.

"On your knees. Let's go!"

I did as I was told. I felt kind of silly out there in the open with my pants down, but I trusted Anthony completely. I could feel his hands examining my lower back and rear end, both of which were intensely sore.

"You've got shrapnel in your butt, Cheese. You're going to need some work, but you'll live."

As Anthony cleaned and bandaged my wounds, I felt something trickling down my face and into my mouth. The metallic taste told me what it was.

"Hey, man," I said. "Think I'm bleeding at this end, too."

The blood on my face freaked me out a bit. I knew I'd suffered a concussion. My ears were ringing, and I had a pounding headache. Maybe I had an open head wound as well. I'd seen a lot of guys get wounded or even killed. But this was my first combat injury, and what they say is true: It's disorienting, painful, and scary.

"Yeah, you've got some shrapnel up here, too," Anthony said, making it sound as simple as a bee sting. "We'll get you cleaned up. You'll be okay."

I started to get woozy. I worried that I was going to pass out in the middle of a mission. But the mission was nearly over.

It turned out that Curt had also taken shrapnel from the grenade blast, so we now had three guys down. And we weren't even in the building yet. The enemy was stronger and heavily armed. That meant calling in a helicopter to evacuate the wounded and bomb the building.

"Everybody, get down," I could hear one of the team leaders say, after we had moved a safe distance away.

Moments later, an Apache helicopter armed with powerful missiles roared overhead. With my head pounding and my back aching, I listened as bombs exploded in the distance.

CHAPTER 22

The first stop was our base in Logar. The docs and nurses evaluated the wounded and determined my injuries to be the least serious. This was correct. Richard was burned on the legs, back, and side from shrapnel. He seemed to be almost unconscious. Curt had a small hole in his chest, which looked nasty but was actually a pretty quick fix. As is sometimes the case, though, the worst damage wasn't visible. This was true of me, as well.

I was wheeled into the medical tent, stripped of my clothes, and given a thorough assessment. There was shrapnel in my buttocks, lower back, leg, arm, and face. They told me I'd be fine, put me to sleep, and cleaned me up.

It was astounding to see and experience the damage that could be done by a single grenade lobbed through a closed window from close range. In a matter of seconds, it had cut down three members of one of the most elite fighting units on the planet. A grenade is an impressive little weapon. It sprays white-hot metal in all directions when it explodes. Even the tiniest fragments can burn through clothing and body armor and embed themselves deep within the victim's tissue. And there's no way to get them all out. The docs removed what they could while I was under anesthesia, but the smaller pieces were left behind. I'd be squeezing them out like pimples for months to come. Eventually, my body would eject just about all the foreign matter. Anything left behind was probably harmless.

Richard and I were shipped to a larger base hospital in Germany for further evaluation. Curt appeared to recover quickly and remained on active duty. But he soon developed complications from a concussion and was sent home.

For me, the concern was basic wound care. Keep everything neat and clean, avoid infection, get back to work. I had more than a dozen wounds. The smallest were like bug bites. The largest, on my buttocks, were the size of quarters. They were deep and painful. I spent nearly two weeks lying flat on my stomach. Tubes were inserted in my wounds to drain fluid and prevent infection.

The hospital staff was great. They appreciated our service and wanted to give us the best treatment. I was uncomfortable, for sure. But pain medication helped. I got to hang out with my fellow wounded buddy as we rested up for what we thought would be a quick return to duty.

We were wrong.

For all three of us, that grenade signaled the end of our deployment, and the beginning of a long struggle with rehabilitation and recovery. I had no idea what I was in for. When you hear the word "shrapnel," you don't realize what it means: months of shuffling around like an old man, attached to tubes and machines; and the nagging sense that something isn't quite right, even as your injuries appear to be healing.

From Germany, I was transferred to Walter Reed National Military Medical Center in Bethesda, Maryland. It was an amazing place. Every single person at Walter Reed seemed 100 percent committed to their job. They were so appreciative of any soldier injured in the line of duty.

My next stop, at a hospital in Virginia, was less impressive. But I did have one great nurse who made the experience tolerable. She helped me understand exactly what was going on with my treatment. She was a pleasant and compassionate person, which is so important when you're recovering from battlefield injuries.

Eventually I went home. The navy flew in my father to spend some time with me, which was a big help. There were still a lot of things I couldn't do for myself. With persistence and daily rehab, I started to improve. Before long I began to feel like my old self again. I was excited. I wanted to get back to work. I was only twenty-eight years old. I figured I had at least a few good years left as an active duty SEAL.

I was wrong.

CHAPTER 23

The migraines started a few months after I got home, in the fall of 2012.

I couldn't figure out what was happening. The wounds had nearly healed. I was ready to start training again. Suddenly, out of the blue, came crippling headaches like nothing I had ever experienced.

They would come on without warning at any time of the day. The pain would start in the back of my neck and then creep upward, until it felt as though my entire head was in a vise grip.

I couldn't think straight.

I couldn't see straight.

All I could do was retreat to the couch or the bedroom and sleep. Sometimes I would get sick to my stomach.

In the beginning, the migraines came once every week or two. Then they began making more frequent visits: twice a week, three times a week . . . four or even five times a week. There were long stretches of time during which I could barely function. It wasn't long before I was transferred to a job that was physically less demanding, working as an instructor for the Training Team. This would allow me to have more time to rest and to make the many medical appointments that clogged my schedule.

But even the instructor's job was often more than I could handle. I was lucky to have great bosses. Most of these men had known me for a long time. They knew something was seriously wrong. I'd always been one of the most reliable guys in the squadron. I wasn't a superstar, but I wasn't a slacker. I didn't complain. I didn't get hurt or sick or injured. I just did my job.

Now?

I was a mess.

There were days when I'd stumble around with one eye closed to guard against the sunlight. My boss would look at me like I was dying.

"Go home, Cheese. Take care of yourself."

"I'm sorry, man. I don't know what's wrong."

He would nod compassionately and send me on my way. And for the rest of the day I'd curl up in a ball while miniature blacksmiths pounded away inside my skull.

Migraines are difficult to diagnose and treat. They can be triggered by a variety of factors, both physical and mental. I was convinced that my headaches were primarily a delayed consequence of the grenade blast in Afghanistan. And maybe they were. But I also understood the power of post-traumatic stress. It can wreak havoc on your body as well as your mind. You try to push it down inside to someplace where you think it can't touch you. But eventually it all boils up to the surface again.

It's a vicious cycle. Stress will cause a physical symptom, like a headache. The headaches then become chronic, and the chronic pain causes depression. And it won't stop until you figure out a way to deal with it. A traumatic brain injury (TBI) adds another layer of complication. In fact, it may be the very first layer, which makes the puzzle even harder to solve. An injury to the brain can cause emotional and psychological symptoms.

In my case, I think it was a combination of factors,

although I have come to believe that TBI was the biggest factor. It isn't just getting hit by a grenade that can cause a brain injury. Years of combat experience expose a SEAL to thousands of concussive blasts. Each door being breached, each missile dropped, can rattle the brain if you're close enough. The damage adds up over time, and there is a price to be paid.

The odds of developing symptoms increase if you experience an obvious head injury. I think that was the case with me. I believe that something happened to my brain when that grenade went off, and it changed me.

I'd spent most of my life acting like nothing bothered me. In fact, almost nothing did bother me. Now I lost my temper easily. I had no patience. And my memory! I couldn't remember a phone number five seconds after it was given to me. I'd forget instructions or miss appointments. Names I'd known well became elusive. I had trouble with simple mental tasks.

I was confused. I was angry.

Let's be honest: I was terrified.

There was a lot of stuff related to my service that I was trying to process. This is common with servicemen and women who suffer combat injuries. I worried about my career coming to an end. I started thinking of friends I had lost in combat. Like Nic Checque, my closest friend. Nic was the one who had gone to Jumpmaster School with me before Operation Neptune Spear. We went through BUD/S together, were drafted by the same squadron, and went on countless missions together. Nic was the closest thing I had to a brother.

On December 8, 2012, Nic was part of a secret mission to rescue an American physician from a heavily guarded compound in eastern Afghanistan. As the first man through the door of a one-room hut where the hostage was being held, Nic was fatally wounded. But his actions allowed other team members to complete the mission and bring the American hostage home alive.

For his bravery, Nic received the Navy Cross, the navy's second-highest award for valor. One of Nic's teammates, Ed Byers, received the Medal of Honor.

I was home in Virginia when I got the news. It was terrible, but strangely familiar. By now I was accustomed to hearing about the passing of my teammates. I'd attended enough funerals and hugged enough teary-eyed parents, wives, and girlfriends. But this was different. Nic wasn't just another SEAL.

He was my best friend.

CHAPTER 24

By the spring of 2013, I was in rough shape. In addition to the headaches and other symptoms, my hair had fallen out after Nic's passing. That was a tough one to explain. Most of the docs thought it was related to stress. It had been nearly a year since I'd been injured, and I had slowly come to the realization that I would never go on another mission.

Although I continued to work on the base, a lot of my time was devoted to chasing a diagnosis for my health issues. I just wanted some relief. But the treatment sometimes felt worse than the illness. I went on a lot of different types of medication to treat headaches and depression. They didn't work very well. They also had a lot of side effects. Some would make me so sleepy I couldn't function. Others would make me anxious or nauseous.

I would never suggest I was mistreated in any way. Every hospital and treatment team did their best. They tried everything. But none of it helped very much.

You know what did help? Stopping by the kennel to play with Cairo.

I know that probably sounds crazy, but it's the truth. Cairo was eight years old by this point. He had lost a step (or two), but he remained one of the smartest and most reliable dogs in the SEAL canine program. Some working dogs lose interest or experience a change in temperament. They suffer so badly from the effects of old age or injury that they can't do the job. Despite nearly getting killed in the line of duty and serving his country for more than five years, this had not happened to Cairo. You could still plug him into almost any mission and get outstanding results.

For that reason, Cairo's retirement was continually pushed back. But it wasn't the only reason. I heard that Cairo might never be allowed to leave the base because of the fame that had come with taking part in Operation Neptune Spear. Now, on the one hand, I sort of understood this. Naval Special Warfare is a highly secretive organization. There is a code of silence and selflessness that comes with serving as a SEAL. The bin Laden mission was the most notable operation in the history of Naval Special Warfare. No one wanted Cairo to be paraded around as some sort of trophy.

On the other hand . . . who cares? It's not like Cairo was going to give up any secrets.

I think the Navy was just concerned about too much attention being placed on Cairo, which in turn would lead to questions about Operation Neptune Spear. The easiest way to deal with this concern was to let Cairo work for as long as possible, and then live out his final days at the kennel. There was nothing wrong with that. As the elder statesman of the kennel, Cairo did not work as much as the primary dogs. And he was well cared for. He was such a good-hearted dog that everyone loved spending time with him. He never lacked for companionship.

Still, I couldn't help but think that he had earned the right to chill at home with Dad. He could eat steak a couple of times a week, run loose in the yard or at the beach, watch television, and sleep wherever he wanted to sleep. Cairo had served his country honorably. He had saved my life and the lives of others. I didn't know how many years he had left. Malinois have a life expectancy of twelve to fifteen years, but obviously Cairo had experienced more stress than a typical dog. It seemed only right that he should have a few happy and relaxing years.

I felt like he needed me, and I sure needed him.

As it became clear that neither one of us was ever again going to set foot in a combat zone, I found myself drawn to Cairo even more than I had been in the past. I'd stop by the kennel two or three times a week, sometimes every day, just to give him a few treats or talk with him. I'd scratch his belly and play fetch with him. It was like hanging out with an old friend.

Sometimes I'd bring Cairo to the office. He wasn't technically my dog. He was still a spare dog, eligible for work. But since most of his time was devoted to lounging around the kennel or doing light training, no one said anything about my frequent visits. Eventually, we all knew he'd be coming home with me. It was only a matter of time.

Or so I hoped.

In the meantime, I settled for long visits. I didn't get to take him home at night, but sometimes I would pick him up and drive to the beach, where there was room to run and play. He seemed to like that. I did, too.

I was still working as an instructor. But I was stuck in a cycle of medication, hospital visits, migraines, and depression.

Spending time with Cairo was the best medicine anyone could have prescribed.

It's hard to explain what he meant to me. I had a Doberman named Sterling at home who was a gentle and lovable fellow. I was also in the process of adopting a Malinois puppy. But Cairo was special. We'd been through something extraordinary together. I didn't think of him merely as a dog.

There were times at home when I would sift through photos of old friends, some long departed, and I'd break down crying. That wasn't me. I'd never been that way. I'd think back to BUD/S, and how I was the guy who never let anything bother him. I was the guy laughing while other guys were crying and quitting.

And now?

Something was very wrong. I just couldn't put my finger on it.

But Cairo helped. Sometimes, after a panic attack or a migraine, I'd stop by the kennel to see him. A sense of calm would overtake me. And it seemed like the same thing would happen to Cairo.

"Yeah, buddy. Dad is here. I'll get you home—promise. Just be patient."

CHAPTER 25

Whenever someone leaves his job as an operator and takes a different role within Naval Special Warfare, he loses touch with some of his teammates. Life goes on. I was stuck in Virginia, working as an instructor, spinning from one doctor's office or hospital to another. Most of my buddies were still training and fighting. I missed them, and I missed my old job, but there was nothing I could do about it. I wasn't allowed on deployment while suffering from chronic migraines. It was too risky.

I was lucky to meet a young woman named Natalie. She was working as a server at a coffee shop in town. She was friendly and pretty, with a nice smile. I'm not exactly the most confident guy when it comes to meeting women, so things moved kind of slowly at first. But I got lucky. She thought my shyness was cute, and eventually she approached me.

"Hey, Will. Would you want to go out sometime?"

"You mean, like, on a date or something?"

"Yeah . . . or something."

I shrugged, smiled. "Sure. That would be great."

Natalie came along at a point when I was about as low as I could be. She didn't run the other way. She understood my attachment to Cairo, and not only fell in love with him but helped me bring him home. I had a lot of good days when Natalie and I first got together, but I had a lot of bad days, too. And she hung in there with me.

In the late fall of 2013, I got word that Cairo was going to be retired. It was way overdue. He'd served long enough. Cairo was eight and a half years old, and his most recent deployment had been cut short because he was suffering from periodontal disease. No dog is perfect, and while Cairo came close, his one genetic weakness was bad teeth. By the time he was retired, more than a dozen of his original teeth had been pulled or broken. He suffered from chronic bad breath, so everyone around him suffered!

Rather than waiting for the Navy to decide what would

happen to Cairo, I made it clear that I still wanted to take him home as soon as he was officially retired.

"He's my dog," I explained. "Always will be. He belongs with me."

I was stationed in Virginia and no longer subject to deployments. I figured there was no reason to deny my request. It was still possible that Cairo's fame might prevent him from leaving the kennel, but I'd heard that was unlikely. The Navy wanted Cairo to have a good home. And what better home than mine?

I didn't get a response right away. Instead, I visited Cairo more often and for longer periods of time. The more time I spent with him, the more I wanted to take him home. It was the right thing to do—for both of us. I figured I would just have to play the waiting game until things worked out.

It wasn't quite that simple.

One afternoon while I was visiting the kennel, I found out that I wasn't the only member of the Cairo fan club.

"You have some competition," I was told by one of the kennel managers.

"What are you talking about?"

"There are a couple other guys who want to take him home."

I did not respond well to this news. Cairo was a terrific

dog, and I could see him having a strong impact on anyone who worked with him. But I was Cairo's first handler and had been through two long deployments with him, as well as years of training. He had saved my life by nearly sacrificing his. I had held him in my arms as he nearly bled to death on the battlefield. We were profoundly connected.

I needed him now, and he needed me. It was as simple as that.

I formally applied to be Cairo's permanent caretaker. This was a process that involved tons of paperwork. I put together my application, and then I sat around and waited. As the weeks and months went by, I became frustrated. I was still dealing with chronic back pain and headaches. I was unhappy with work and missed my friends. I felt like Cairo would ease some of that discomfort. I visited him several times a week. After a while I started to get these crazy thoughts. I'd sit there at the kennel and talk to Cairo.

"You know what, buddy? I'm gonna take you out of here. We'll run off somewhere and hide. Just me and you."

This would not have worked out well for anyone. Not for me, not for the navy, and not for Cairo. And I never would have gone through with it. But it's an indication of my emotional state at the time that I even thought about it.

A few months after I submitted the paperwork, there was

movement. The guys who ran the dog program interviewed each person who had applied to adopt Cairo (there were three of us, I believe). The interview included a lot of basic questions to ensure that Cairo would be cared for in a safe and appropriate manner.

Q: Where will he sleep?

A: With me.

Q: What will he eat?

A: Mostly steak, but whatever he wants.

Q: What are you going to do with him?

A: Well, pretty much everything. It's not like I got a lot else going on.

Q: Why do you want him?

A: Because I love him. He's my dog.

There were other questions, none of which were hard for me to answer. The interview lasted about thirty to forty-five minutes and was conducted by someone I considered to be a friend. But he did not show any favoritism. He was polite but formal, which was fine. He had a job to do, and he did it well. I respected his position. When it was over, we stood and shook hands.

"How long before you make a decision?" I asked.

He smiled. "You know the Navy, Will. Things don't move quickly."

I laughed. "Copy that."

A few days went by. Nothing. A week. Two weeks. A month.

Almost every day I would stop by the kennel to see Cairo. I would hand-feed him and play with him. He was approaching nine years old, and although he still looked fit, he did seem to be slowing down. He wasn't quite as eager to run around or play. His mood was fine. He just seemed to be a little more laid-back.

Once in a while, I'd ask my friends at the kennel if they had heard anything about the adoption process. The answer was always the same.

"Nothing yet. Sorry."

I tried not to make a pest of myself. For one thing, I didn't want my nagging to have a negative impact on the process. Second, this was life in the military. The decision was being made at several levels above my buddies at the kennel. I'm sure everyone wanted what was best for Cairo, but the waiting caused me a lot of sleepless nights.

Finally, one afternoon in April 2014, I got a phone call at work. It was my friend from the kennel, the same guy who had conducted the interview.

"Hey, Cheese. The orders came through."

"For Cairo?"

He laughed. "Yeah, why else would I be calling?"

I paused for a moment to let it sink in. I have never been the most emotional guy, but at that moment, I could barely catch my breath.

"He's mine?"

"Sure looks that way. You just have to come by and finish the paperwork."

"On my way," I said. Then I dropped the office phone, grabbed my cell, and typed out a quick text to Natalie. My hands were shaking as I fumbled over the keypad.

"HE'S COMING HOME!"

I checked out of work early, drove straight to the kennel, and began filling out the required forms. Not surprisingly, there was a lot of paperwork. You can't request a new stapler in the navy without filling out a bunch of forms. Adopting the most famous military working dog in history? Well, that takes some time.

Once the paperwork was completed, I walked out of the office and into the kennel, where Cairo sat quietly in his cage. As usual, he stood up and began wagging his tail. He let out a soft "Woof!" which was just his way of saying hello. Cairo was accustomed to my visits by now, so he knew the drill. He'd be let out for a while, and we'd play together, maybe go for a walk or have something to eat.

I took a seat on the ground as he trotted into my arms. Then I hooked up his harness and led him to the parking lot. As we walked out of the kennel for the last time, I couldn't help but smile.

"No more metal box for you."

I threw open the door to my truck. Cairo jumped into the passenger side of the cab and curled up contentedly. I turned the key. As the engine rumbled, I reached over and gave him a scratch behind the ears.

"One stop on the way home."

Cairo pushed his head against my hand and growled warmly.

"Steak for dinner," I said. "Hope you don't mind."

CHAPTER 26

It was a surprise to discover that I wasn't the only one in the house suffering from PTSD.

The signs were subtle at first, like the way Cairo preferred not to be left alone. He was totally comfortable for the first couple of days, probably because I took him everywhere with me. Then I started to notice that if I walked from the kitchen to the living room, Cairo would get up and follow. If I went outside, he would stand at the door and scratch the screen. Then he would whine or bark until I let him out. Once he was with me, everything was fine. He'd trail alongside, happy and content.

But the surest clue came about a week after he came home.

A big spring storm rolled through the area. I was sitting in the living room when I noticed Cairo panting. Then he started pacing nervously around the room, with his tongue hanging out and drool falling from his muzzle.

"What's the matter?" I said.

Cairo walked over and jumped up on the couch. He pushed his head into my hands but refused to lie down. Instead, he stood on the sofa for a moment, trembling and panting, and then jumped right back down and resumed pacing.

"What's wrong with him?" Natalie asked.

"I have no idea. I've never seen him do anything like this before."

Cairo walked to one of the windows and stared outside. Then he went to the door. I stood up and followed him, thinking he heard something in the backyard. I couldn't imagine what that might be. It wasn't like we got a lot of wild animals in our neighborhood. Even if there had been a coyote or some other visitor, the Cairo I knew would merely have been excited.

Not terrified.

I looked out the window. The late afternoon sky was growing dark in a way that signals the unmistakable approach of rough weather. Off in the distance, I heard a rumble of thunder. It didn't last long, and it wasn't very loud. Nonetheless, it provoked in Cairo an immediate response: He cowered under the dining room table.

"Oh no," I said to Natalie. "He's afraid of the thunderstorm."

She felt terrible for Cairo. But as someone who had only been exposed to ordinary dogs, she didn't think it was a big deal. Lots of dogs are spooked by loud noises.

"Has he always been like this?" she asked innocently.

I shook my head in disbelief. "Uhhh . . . no."

That was an understatement. Cairo was a fearless dog who would run into a gunfight without hesitation. He would sit calmly in the back of a helicopter as it was shaken by wind or danced out of the way of RPG fire. He'd been shot at nearly point-blank range and still not given up the fight. He'd held his ground as grenades rattled the earth around him.

Nothing bothered Cairo.

Nothing!

But I suppose there was a price to pay for all that he endured. A lot of the stuff I experienced didn't faze me in the least—until I came home and had to live in the "normal" world. After a decade of training, fighting, and living with one purpose, I struggled as I tried to figure out a *new* purpose. The constant noise in my head and the persistent, inexplicable physical pain that went along with it made the adjustment even harder.

It messed me up. And obviously it had affected Cairo, as well.

"Come here, boy," I said, coaxing him out from under the table. "Everything will be okay."

For the most part, it was. We learned to deal with the thunderstorms. Although he often would end up sleeping in my bed, I gave Cairo his own room and his own bed. If a storm happened to roll through in the middle of the night, Cairo usually would wake in a puddle of his own urine. We'd have to sit with him and calm him down until the storm passed. Then we'd toss his bedding into the laundry and give him a different place to sleep.

There was no point in correcting any of this behavior. He wasn't trying to be troublesome. He was just scared out of his wits by something that had never frightened him in the past. Something that presented no threat to his safety. If that's not PTSD, then I don't know what is.

Getting Cairo home was one of the happiest times of my life (and I hope his as well), but there was a period of transition for both of us. Like many recent retirees, Cairo struggled with boredom and restlessness. It took a while for him to settle in at home. As a handler, I had been Cairo's teammate, but I was also his boss. I was Dad, and like any dad, I tried to balance affection with discipline. On deployment, we both knew our roles. Now that he was no longer working, and clearly scarred by his years of service, I was reluctant to be hard on him.

Any dog will take advantage of that situation if you let him. The smarter and more strong-willed the animal is, the more likely you are to find yourself in a turf war. And a Belgian Malinois is very smart and strong-willed!

For the first few weeks that Cairo was home, I let him do pretty much whatever he wanted. I was grateful to have him around, and he was happy to no longer be living in a cage. One day on the way home from work, I stopped to pick up a tuna sandwich. When I got home, Cairo was wandering around the house. I gave him a hug, then set the sandwich on a table in the living room before going into the kitchen to grab something to drink. I'm not sure what I was thinking.

Anyway, when I walked back into the living room, Cairo was lying on the floor with the sandwich between his front paws. Tuna fish and mayonnaise covered his snout.

"Cairo," I said. "Come on, man."

I didn't scold him. After all, this was mostly my fault. I'd left the sandwich out in plain view, easily accessible. How could Cairo resist? He had been living in a kennel, where gifts such as this rarely presented themselves. I was upset about losing my meal, but it was an impressive bit of thievery. In a matter of minutes Cairo had managed to remove about two feet of plastic wrap from the sandwich. Most dogs would have devoured the whole thing and either spit out the plastic or pooped it out later. Not Cairo. He somehow removed the wrapping. And rather than eating the sandwich quickly, he had licked out the tuna and cheese from the middle.

When I caught him in the act (or right after the act), he looked up at me impishly.

"What's the big deal, Dad? I left you the best part."

CHAPTER 27

After a month or so, we got into a nice rhythm. Cairo was no longer a working dog, so there was no need to do any hard-core training. But the truth is, he loved working, so I had to keep him busy. I tried to mix some of the more interesting and fun aspects of his old life into his new life. No more gunfire or explosions. No more bite work. But plenty of fetch and running on the beach or in open fields.

Unfortunately, the slight hitch in his step progressed to a limp that was noticeable after a few minutes of retrieving balls. No surprise. He was almost ten years old. He had a metal plate in his leg. Even without the injury, Cairo would have experienced the effects of arthritis, just like any other aging combat veteran. The job beats you up. But his drive to work and run remained strong. Cairo would never quit a game of fetch. He would push right through the pain. It was up to me to keep him from getting too banged up.

Life was pretty good for most of that summer. Cairo spent a lot of time lazing around the house, being loved not just by me and Natalie but by everyone who visited. In anticipation of Cairo coming home, I had bought a motorcycle with a sidecar. I liked to ride bikes in nice weather and thought it might be cool to share the experience with Cairo. Turns out, he loved it!

We used to get some great looks from people as we rode around town together. Cairo would sit in the sidecar, wearing a helmet and doggles, with his mouth open, trying to catch the wind. He liked going out on my boat, as well. Cairo had never been much of a water dog. By that I mean he wasn't a swimmer. Didn't even like getting wet in the rain. But he enjoyed sitting on my boat as it rocked in the waves, and we spent endless hours doing exactly that.

With few dietary restrictions and a more relaxed exercise regimen, Cairo naturally began to lose a little bit of his lean-ness. I wouldn't exactly say we "fattened him up," but if you had seen him in his prime, you would have noticed the difference. He no longer had the look of a world-class athlete. Instead, he looked . . . healthy. Content. He was leading a life of leisure, just as he deserved.

Still, there were issues even on the best days. Cairo suffered from separation anxiety. The fact that he liked to follow me around was no big deal. More challenging was the destruction Cairo would sometimes cause when we left him home alone. Every time I would drive away, I'd see Cairo's head appear in one of the front windows. Sometimes he'd just sit there and wait. Other times I'd return to find the blinds pulled from their rods or chewed into pieces. While this behavior was frustrating (and expensive!), it was not malicious. He wanted to know where I was, and when I'd return. In Cairo's mind, a better view would provide some of the answers. It was simply a matter of insecurity.

For a while we tried confining him to a spare bedroom when we left. That didn't work at all. He would destroy the entire room. The next step, unfortunately, was to confine him to a crate when we were out of the house. That lasted only a few days before he figured out how to escape. Eventually, I used a sheet of plexiglass to make the crate almost escape-proof.

Almost . . .

Meaning, sometimes he got out; sometimes he didn't.

I guess you could say Cairo won the war if not every battle, since we ultimately decided that it was best to leave him alone as little as possible. For the most part, wherever we went, Cairo tagged along.

Cairo and I didn't always get along in retired life. Even though he was a sweet, big-hearted dog, we had our disagreements. Retired or not, he was still a combat assault dog. I had to keep that in mind. He was never aggressive, just increasingly unwilling to do what he was told. I had to take responsibility for this because I was his handler. I knew better. You can't let an alpha dog like Cairo act like he's in charge. Even as an old-timer, he'll be more than a handful.

Cairo was affectionate with others, but not always obedient. Part of this stemmed from the fact that everyone was naturally attracted to Cairo. He was handsome and friendly, with an almost majestic appearance. The combination of being physically intimidating and personally charming allowed him to get away with a lot. Sometimes I would have to go beyond a simple verbal correction. If he didn't do what he was told, I'd put him in his kennel for a few minutes, just to get the point across.

But we always made up in the end. I loved Cairo and he loved me. Nothing would ever change that.

The Belgian Malinois as a breed is known to be prickly around unfamiliar dogs. But we never had a problem with Cairo. He coexisted peacefully with our Doberman, Sterling, and with Hagen, a female Malinois who was still a puppy. Hagen was excitable and energetic. To Cairo, she was endlessly annoying, forcing play sessions that didn't interest him in the least. But he never protested. Instead, he'd just lie on the floor while Hagen bounced around, pawing at Cairo, jumping on his back, even nipping at his neck. The first few times this happened, I pulled Hagen away—for her own good! After a while I didn't even bother to intervene. I just let them play. Not once did Cairo display any aggression toward Hagen. Somehow, he knew that it was all just fun and games.

One time we drove to Florida to visit Natalie's family. They had a bulldog that was generally well behaved and friendly, especially with humans, but she didn't like sharing her toys with other dogs. At one point, the dogs were outside playing, when Cairo tried to run down a ball. The bulldog didn't like that. As Cairo went after the ball, the bulldog went after Cairo.

The bulldog leaped at Cairo with a growl and clamped its jaws down around Cairo's leg. Cairo was softened by age and injuries, but he still could have ripped the bulldog to pieces.

Incredibly, Cairo barely even responded to the attack. He shook the bulldog off, dropped the ball, and meekly walked away. He didn't yelp, didn't bark, didn't even growl. It was like he barely even noticed, or simply couldn't be bothered to respond.

Well, this isn't worth my time.

A few minutes later, I noticed that Cairo was limping—and it wasn't the usual little hitch that I knew so well.

"Come here, buddy," I said, clapping my hands. Cairo jogged over slowly and stood in front of me. I ran my hands over his leg and felt something wet. Sure enough, Cairo was bleeding. I pulled his fur back to get a better look. The wound was at least two inches long.

"Gotta get him to the vet," I said. "He might need a few stitches."

Even for Cairo, this was remarkable. He had barely reacted to having his leg cut open. To say he had mellowed with age would be an understatement. He was a gentle old soul now. He was a lover, not a fighter.

Retirement agreed with Cairo, and I sort of envied him. By this point I had come to terms with the approaching end of my own navy career. Some guys evolve naturally from operator to instructor or even commander. Not me. I had been drawn to the SEALs because I wanted to be in the action. I wanted to test myself under the most rigorous conditions. If that was taken away from me, then my career was over. I had no interest in a more sedentary form of service.

To be honest, I wasn't healthy enough for any job. I still suffered from back pain and headaches. I had crippling bouts of anxiety that would come on in waves. Having Cairo around helped improve my mood, but the truth was, it was time for me to move on.

Separating from the SEALs is not the simplest thing. If you've got twenty years under your belt and you're in decent physical and emotional shape, then you simply retire and collect your pension.

I was only thirty years old, with twelve years of service. I'd given everything I had to my country and my brothers. But like Cairo, I was now damaged goods. In my current state, I had nothing left to offer. I just wanted to get better and then figure out what to do with the rest of my life. So I applied for a medical retirement from the navy, a process that can be slow and complicated.

I have no complaints about my time as a SEAL. I served alongside some incredible people and learned from generous and talented mentors. When my health began to deteriorate, I was lucky to have the support of bosses who knew that I was in pain. Everyone wanted to help. It's just that no one really knew how.

Having Cairo home was more beneficial than any other type of therapy or treatment. Unfortunately, we were separated again after just a few months, when the navy suggested I undergo treatment for substance abuse.

There had been a lot of concern on the part of my friends and coworkers. They saw how badly I was struggling. They saw how much pain I was in. Their intervention was a display of love and support.

So I went through a treatment program. I wanted to get better—for myself, and for the people I loved.

And for Cairo.

CHAPTER 28

Dogs throw up. A lot.

That's not news to anyone who has ever owned a dog for even the shortest time. Dogs are messy. They poop and pee and puke. Sometimes in the house. In fact, I've known a lot of people who have given up dogs because they didn't want to deal with some of the sights and smells that are part of the bargain.

I always thought it was a small price to pay. You get used to it after a while.

With a little training, most dogs adapt to a schedule. Get up in the morning, eat breakfast, go for a walk. Clean out the system. Not much different from their owners, really. Vomiting is not part of the daily program, but it doesn't usually signify anything serious. Dogs eat all kinds of disgusting stuff they are not supposed to eat: garbage, roadkill, mushrooms, dirt, even other dogs' poop. Just about any of these things can make a dog sick. But in most cases, the dog feels better almost immediately afterward.

Cairo had been raised in a bubble. He was carefully trained and sensibly fed. He had never been much of a scrounger when it came to food. He was a healthy dog, so when he began throwing up frequently in the late fall of 2014, I took notice. The first time it happened, I found Cairo in the kitchen, standing over a small puddle of yellowish liquid. I thought perhaps he'd peed on the floor, which would have been strange enough. But it was too small a puddle, and the look on Cairo's face reflected queasiness.

"What's up, pal? You okay?"

Upon closer inspection, I could see that Cairo had thrown up a small amount of bile. This struck me as odd, but I shrugged it off and cleaned up the mess. Then I took Cairo for a walk. He was a little woozy and needed a nap afterward, but otherwise okay. By that night he was back to his old friendly, happy self. I chalked it up to heartburn (or whatever it is that dogs get that feels like heartburn) and forgot all about it.

Until a couple of days later, when it happened again.

And a week after that, when he threw up his dinner less than an hour after eating.

"Something's wrong," I said to Natalie. "This isn't like him."

Since Cairo was a retired military working dog who had spent his entire career with the SEALs, I figured I could just take him to one of the veterinarians at the base. They were happy to help, but an examination turned up nothing.

"He's getting old," the doc said. "It's perfectly normal. I wouldn't worry about it."

Cleaning up after Cairo became a common part of our routine. But most of the time he seemed just fine. A bit less energetic, maybe, but not "sick."

In December, Natalie and I began making plans for a holiday trip. I had always wanted to visit the National September 11 Memorial and Museum (also known as the "9/11 Memorial") in New York City. Although I still suffered from migraines and back pain, and my mood varied from day to day, it's fair to say that I had improved somewhat, and my medical retirement was moving forward. I certainly didn't feel like my old self, but I did feel . . . *better*.

I wasn't sure how I'd be affected by the 9/11 Memorial. You might think that every SEAL would have visited at some point, as the 9/11 Memorial is directly related to the idea of fighting terrorism. But that isn't true. For me, it seemed like there was never enough time. I used my vacations to get away from the stress of work. I didn't need to be reminded of the horror and tragedy of 9/11. I knew precisely what had happened. I lived with the fallout every day. I devoted my life to ensuring that nothing like it ever happened again.

But now that I was no longer deploying, I felt a gnawing sense of curiosity. Natalie and I had never been to New York City. We began making plans to visit the 9/11 Memorial and celebrate New Year's Eve in Times Square. To make things even more interesting, we decided to take Cairo and Hagen with us. Sterling we left with a friend. Three dogs in New York City was more than even I was willing to tackle.

We loaded up the car and left Virginia on December 29. A seven-hour ride felt more like twelve hours because Cairo vomited twice along the way. Cairo had traveled all over the world—by car, plane, helicopter, and boat. He rarely suffered from motion sickness, so his sudden and persistent nausea was distressing, but it wasn't exactly a shock.

In addition to his ongoing stomach issues, Cairo had

exhibited some unusual behavior in the days leading up to the trip. For one thing, he had no interest in playing; he simply wanted to lie around the house and sleep. I also caught him eating dog poop in the backyard. I don't know if it was his own poop or if it belonged to Sterling or Hagen. Not that it matters. I'd known Cairo since he was three years old, and I had never seen him do this. I was so surprised that I didn't even yell at him when it happened. I just sort of walked over and pulled him away.

"What are you doing, boy? That stuff will make you sick."

It sure did. The first time Cairo vomited, we were crossing into Delaware on I-95. Fortunately, we always carried a few towels in the car. Natalie grabbed one and turned around just in time to give him a target. The second time was somewhere on the New Jersey Turnpike. Same thing. I felt sorry for Natalie, but she didn't complain; she was just worried about Cairo.

Despite all the adventures I had experienced in the previous decade, I still got excited as we crossed the George Washington Bridge and entered Manhattan. I'd seen a good chunk of the world, but I remained a country boy at heart, and there is nothing like New York City to make a country boy feel wide-eyed. The sheer scope of the city is remarkable—so many people, skyscrapers, cars, and buses, all crammed into one little patch of land. It's a wonder the place works at all.

The week between Christmas and New Year's is among the busiest of the year in New York. We tried to relax and not get all stressed out about the traffic or the crowds. It was all part of the experience. By the time we pulled up to our hotel near Central Park, Cairo was lethargic from car sickness and the long ride. Hagen, who was barely a year old, bounced excitedly around the car.

A lot of hotels do not accept dogs. But since Cairo was a retired service dog and Hagen was a working dog in training, we were usually allowed to take them with us wherever we went. Still, we didn't want to pull up to a crowded hotel in Manhattan, with thousands of people nearby, and let two big Malinois hop out of the car.

I pulled into the valet parking lane, put the car in park, and asked Natalie to wait with the dogs. Then I got out and explained the situation to the valet.

"We have a couple big dogs here," I said. "They're friendly and well trained, and we'll have them leashed. The hotel knows we're coming."

The valet smiled warily and peeked into the window of the car.

"Ummmm . . . no problem, sir."

We emptied the car, checked in, and went up to our room. As we walked into the lobby, some people stopped and stared. It takes a lot to get someone's attention in Manhattan, but Cairo and Hagen were both beautiful dogs. Several people approached and asked if they could get a closer look, or maybe even pet the dogs. They were both muzzled, so we said sure. Even people who were clearly afraid of dogs—or at least these two dogs— stared in wonder. I guess it was like looking at a lion in the zoo: Even if you're scared, you can't help but admire the animal.

Over the next couple of days, we took Hagen almost everywhere. She was so easygoing and friendly, and she loved interacting with people, especially in the park. She was a puppy who had not been trained to bite or attack. She could be trusted around crowds. We had only one minor incident with her on that trip, when someone accidentally stepped on her foot. Like any dog, Hagen could be unpredictable when hurt, but she barely registered anything more than mild surprise. Still, it taught us to be sensitive to our surroundings. New York is a beautiful and vibrant city, but it's a challenge for anyone visiting with a large dog—or two large dogs.

Sadly, Cairo didn't get to see much of it. He was pretty sick for the first couple of days. We took him outside only to go to the bathroom. Although he stopped throwing up by the second day, he lacked energy. He just didn't seem like himself. We didn't want to test him around strangers when he wasn't feeling well, and he seemed content to hang out in the hotel room.

By the morning of December 31, the crowds had begun to swell. It didn't seem like such a great idea to take Cairo or Hagen to Times Square. We decided to move to a different hotel where we'd have a view of the Times Square New Year's Eve celebration from our room on an upper floor. We ordered takeout food for dinner, and the four of us curled up together on a king-sized bed. When the ball dropped in Times Square, we pressed our faces against the window and watched it fall. We counted down the seconds as 2014 gave way to 2015.

It was a nice night.

Two days later, on January 2, we drove to Lower Manhattan and visited the 9/11 Memorial. I wanted to take Cairo. I wanted to share the experience with him. I know he would not have understood, but for me, Cairo's presence was important. It just seemed . . . *appropriate.*

Unfortunately, while Cairo was no longer getting sick, he still seemed tired and disinterested. He wasn't a problem. But I'd done enough research on the 9/11 Memorial to know that it was going to be crowded. I didn't think it was fair to put Cairo through an experience like that if he wasn't feeling well.

We did take Hagen, and she behaved well. It was nice to have her with us, but it would have been even better with Cairo. The tragedy of 9/11 had led to our coming together. We were partners ten years later, tethered together on the ground in Pakistan, when the man responsible for the atrocity of 9/11 was finally brought to justice.

I needed to see the memorial, to experience it firsthand. And I wanted Cairo to be there with me. He just wasn't up to it.

Even without Cairo, the memorial was a profoundly moving experience. I suppose that's true for anyone who visits. But it's compounded by an emotional connection to the event itself, or to events that have arisen in its wake.

I can't imagine what it's like to walk through the 9/11 Memorial if you lost a loved one on that day. It was hard enough for me just to see the names of people who perished, and to think of the way some of those people died. They had to make a choice between jumping from the ninetieth floor of a building or burning within its walls. I thought of the first responders who rushed to the site and selflessly gave their lives.

And I thought of the brothers I had lost over the years, men who had died while fighting an endless and often thankless war sparked by 9/11.

I remember feeling so overwhelmed that I couldn't speak. I remember feeling like I wanted to cry, but not being able to shed a tear. I remember feeling a profound mix of sadness and pride as I stood in front of a display case devoted to Operation Neptune Spear. There was a brick from the compound where Osama bin Laden was found; a long-sleeved camouflage jersey worn by a SEAL on the night of the raid (the owner was unidentified, but I knew it belonged to Rob O'Neill).

I didn't say a word.

I remember reaching down and giving Hagen a hug, and wishing that Cairo was by her side.

CHAPTER 29

Through the windshield of my Toyota Tundra, I watched as the mountains of Tennessee and Arkansas gave way to the flatland of Oklahoma and the Texas Panhandle. Cairo sat next to me. He was a comfortable copilot, as usual. We'd seen a lot of the country together over the years, much of it from the cab of a truck. I like driving. You can relax and let the road unspool at its own leisurely pace.

Our destination was a small town in Colorado, where my friend Jack lived. He was a retired SEAL. We went through BUD/S together. Jack had invited me to stay at his place while I worked at a security internship nearby. By this point it had become clear that I would be separating from the navy. But the process for a medical retirement was slow, with endless paperwork, interviews, and therapy.

It was a frustrating time. I had been wounded in the spring of 2012. It was now late February of 2015. While there had been some sputtering progress toward recovery, I frequently walked around like a zombie. I was plagued by headaches, back pain, and memory loss. I still wrestled with bouts of sadness and depression. In my more selfish moments, I got angry.

I gave twelve years to the navy. I'm proud of my service and I wouldn't trade it for anything. But please . . . let me move on.

I had a lot of friends and bosses who patiently rode out my bad days and gave me support. But life goes on. Most of my closest friends and teammates were either still in the grinding cycle of training and deployment or they had retired; a few, of course, had died.

Meanwhile, I was in what felt like a permanent holding pattern.

Fortunately, there were other opportunities, like the internship in Colorado, which would be followed by another internship in Iowa. Both of them involved dog training programs. This was a chance to explore the civilian world. I was excited and grateful. But I wasn't sure what to do about Cairo. I would be on the road for roughly a month, and I felt bad about leaving Natalie at home with three dogs. Cairo was not his old self. But he had rallied somewhat since our trip to New York, so I decided to take him with me.

I didn't know what else to do. Like me, Cairo seemed to have good days and bad days. He could go for a walk or play fetch and seem perfectly fine in the morning. Then in the afternoon, he might be sick or exhausted. Not every day, mind you, but often enough that it remained worrisome. I regularly brought him in to see the base veterinarian. He kept giving me the same message: He's an old dog and he's been through a lot.

Malinois sometimes live to the ripe old age of thirteen or fourteen, especially if they come from good stock, are well cared for, and get lucky. Cairo was impeccably bred. Everyone took care of him and loved him. But he had endured a lot of trauma and stress. It made sense that he was feeling the effects of that now.

Still, I worried that there was something else bothering him. I became a nuisance by taking Cairo to the vet a couple of times a month, or even weekly. This was a problem, and not merely because the vet didn't think there was anything wrong with Cairo. He was no longer a military working dog. He had been retired, which meant he was ineligible for unlimited free care by navy docs. That might seem unfair, considering Cairo's record. But that's the way it was.

"Will, you're going to have to find an outside vet," the doc told me. "You can't keep bringing him here."

Cairo tolerated the cross-country trip reasonably well. We made it from Virginia to Colorado in three days. He got sick only once along the way. But it wasn't long after we arrived that Cairo started to go downhill. He seemed more tired than usual. He didn't want to interact with my friend Jack. For the first few days, all he did was sleep. I thought he was having trouble adjusting to the altitude of the Rockies, but when he began throwing up, I grew more concerned. Cairo was losing weight. He seemed even sicker than he had been before we went to New York.

"I'm worried about him," I said to Jack. "I think he needs to see someone."

Jack agreed. "Let me make a call."

I was lucky. Jack was friends with a local civilian vet. He explained the symptoms, and the doc said to bring Cairo right in.

The vet took some X-rays, which revealed issues with Cairo's stomach and digestive system. But the results were inconclusive. In order to find out what was really going on, he needed to perform surgery. It was scary but necessary.

"There's obviously something very wrong," the doc said. "But I can't give you any definitive answers without operating."

When the vet found out that Cairo was a retired working dog, he offered to do the work free of charge. He had no idea that this was the *famous* Cairo. But he refused to take payment and did the entire procedure and follow-up appointments out of the kindness of his heart. The gratitude I have for such a person . . . well, I cannot put it into words. People like that are hard to find.

After the surgery, the vet came right out to explain what he had found. It was complicated, and not encouraging.

Cairo was so bloated that his spleen had been displaced. It had "flipped" over his stomach and gotten lodged between the stomach wall and other vital organs. Dogs have a simple digestive system that usually causes no problems. But when something goes wrong, the results can be catastrophic. The very description of Cairo's malady made me queasy. It also made me feel so sorry for him. I could just imagine what he had gone through for the past several months, and how uncomfortable he must have been.

Fortunately, Cairo made it out of the surgery without any complications. The doc said he was able to put everything back in its proper place. The prognosis was as good as it could be given Cairo's age and history. The best thing for him now, the doc said, was plenty of rest.

For the next two weeks, I slept with Cairo in Jack's

basement. Whenever I wasn't working, I was right by his side. Jack had to leave town for a while, but his wife and kids were kind enough to let me stay in their home. They took care of me and Cairo while he was recovering. Although he lacked much of an appetite, he seemed to be doing okay.

Eventually, I loaded up the truck and headed to Iowa for my second internship. While I enjoyed the work, my heart wasn't really into it. I worried about Cairo. He seemed to do better for a few days, then began deteriorating again. The vet had warned me to look for bloating in Cairo's midsection. This would be an indication that he was retaining water and that his digestive system was acting up.

One morning, he threw up. Afterward, I ran my hands along his belly. I found nothing unusual. In fact, he seemed to be the opposite of bloated. I could feel his ribs sticking out.

"What's the matter?" I said as Cairo lowered his head into my chest and tried to snuggle.

In late March, I decided to hit the road. The internship was not over, but Cairo was clearly sick. I wanted to get him home.

We made it to Virginia in two days, driving roughly ten hours a day. Cairo did not appear to be in great distress, but neither was he the happy copilot I had come to know and love. I'd scratch him behind the ears, pat him on the head. Sometimes he'd look up at me or roll over as if to ask for more, but mainly he just slept.

I thought that being in his own home would do Cairo some good. Maybe he would start eating more and naturally recuperate. This was not the case. Within a couple of days he had stopped eating completely.

I decided to take him to a vet who command had been using on and off for a long time. He was mainly a civilian vet, but he had also done some work for dogs on the base. When we arrived at the hospital, a receptionist told us the doctor was going to be in surgery all day.

"Would you mind seeing one of the other doctors?"

I looked at Natalie. She shrugged. What choice did we have? Cairo was obviously very sick. His weight had dipped to fifty-five pounds, and he had trouble holding his head up. His eyes were sunken and hollow.

"Of course," I said. "No problem. Thanks for squeezing us in."

The doctor examined Cairo thoroughly. She gave him an injection of medicine to stop the vomiting. Then she suggested we take him home to rest. He'd been through surgery and was on the road for a month. It wasn't surprising that he was sick. The recovery would take time, she said.

We agreed to take him home and pamper him, and to bring him back in a few days if there was no improvement. But just as we were getting ready to leave, the other doctor walked into the waiting room, fresh out of surgery.

We shook hands and made small talk for a few minutes. Then he began examining Cairo. The doctor had known Cairo for a long time, and I could tell by the look on his face that he was concerned.

"You know," he said. "Let's get some X-rays and start him on some fluids."

The scans revealed bad news. There was a large mass in Cairo's stomach. But there was no way to determine the nature of the mass without opening him up. Heavily invasive surgery.

Again.

It seemed so cruel. Cairo hadn't even come close to recovering from the previous surgery. I worried that he wasn't strong enough to go through it again. But what choice did we have?

"Okay," I told the doc. "Do what you have to do."

He agreed that Cairo was too weak to endure another surgical procedure right away. My job was to take Cairo home and help him get stronger. Soon enough, he'd be ready for surgery.

Eating was important, so Natalie and I blended Cairo's food and fed him through a syringe. We gave him intravenous fluids and lots of medication. We nursed him, slept with him, and told him how much we loved him. Sometimes Hagen or Sterling would try to get him to play, but Cairo had no interest. For the most part, they were nice enough to leave him alone.

After a few days, Cairo showed minor improvement. He still had no interest in eating on his own, but by pushing fluids and force feeding, we were able to put a few pounds on him. When I brought him to the vet on the morning of his surgery, he seemed to be in decent spirits. There was even a slight bounce in his step as we walked up to the door. I remember feeling bad for him. He had no idea what was coming. At the same time, I tried to be hopeful.

"We're going to get you all fixed up, buddy. Don't worry."

I gave him a hug and handed the leash to one of the three cheerful young women who worked the front counter. Then I walked away without looking back.

For the next several hours, I tried to make the time pass without worrying. It was impossible. In the early afternoon, I got a phone call. Cairo had made it through surgery and was ready to be picked up. The doctor would go over what he found when we got there.

Natalie and I hopped into my truck and drove as fast as we could to the vet hospital. When they brought Cairo out, he was still woozy from the surgery. I was just happy he was alive. As we waited in an examining room, the doctor came in to talk with us. I could tell by his serious demeanor that the news was not good. In addition to the mass that had shown up on the X-ray, the surgery revealed that Cairo's stomach wall was about ten times thicker than normal. The doctor had taken tissue samples so that a biopsy could be performed. The test results would be available in a few days.

He never once used the word "cancer," but just by the way everyone was acting, I could tell the prognosis was poor.

"What do we do now?" I asked.

"Same as before," he said. "Take him home. Feed him, give him fluids, try to make him comfortable."

He urged us to have faith. He told us not to jump to any conclusions. I appreciated the effort, but I did not find it to be a convincing speech.

CHAPTER 30

Cairo came home on March 31, 2015. My birthday. He was in rough shape but very much alive. Maybe, I thought, he'll be okay. After all, this wasn't his first rodeo. Cairo had been sick before. He'd been shot. He was no ordinary dog. He could survive anything.

We celebrated my thirty-first birthday that night. Just me and Natalie and the dogs. A quiet evening at home. As much as possible, we tried to include Cairo, but he wasn't in a partying mood. None of us were.

That night, Cairo slept in his favorite dog bed. I slept on the floor next to him and tried to make sure he was comfortable. Every so often he would roll over and groan. In the middle of the night I heard a sound. I woke to find Cairo crouching, his legs quivering. I moved my head just in time to avoid being sprayed with diarrhea.

Even after he was done, the cramping went on for several minutes. I kept a hand on his back until the spasms passed. Finally, he slumped to the floor.

"I'm sorry, pal," was all I could offer. Natalie and I cleaned up the room, and then we all went back to bed.

Three days passed in a haze of sickness and mess. The vomiting and diarrhea were relentless. Cairo would throw up or go to the bathroom everywhere. He would whimper and cry. Then he would fall asleep with his head on my lap. A little while later, the cycle would repeat itself. The poor guy seemed to be in so much pain.

It finally got to the point where we couldn't take it anymore, so we brought him back to the vet. They wanted to weigh him when we arrived, but Cairo could barely stand on the scale. I had to hold him in place. He was a bag of bones by that point, his weight having dropped to slightly more than fifty pounds. At his peak, he had weighed between seventy and seventy-five pounds, so he'd lost nearly a third of his mass.

The doctor who had operated on Cairo was tied up in

surgery when we arrived, so we saw his associate again. She was compassionate and soft-spoken as she looked him over and delivered the news. The biopsy was positive. Cairo had cancer. Advanced.

"Is there any chance he could recover?" I asked.

She shook her head sadly.

"I'm sorry. No."

I looked at Natalie. She was sitting with Cairo on the floor, rubbing his back and trying not to cry.

Okay . . . Enough.

It was time to let him go. We had reached the point where we were keeping Cairo alive not for him but for us. We were being selfish. He had experienced an unreasonable amount of pain, and it was only going to get worse.

The doctor agreed with our decision. Actually, it was 100 percent my decision. It would not have been fair to ask Natalie to decide. Cairo had risked his life for me. I could never repay him. But I could end his suffering. That was my responsibility, and mine alone. It was heartbreaking, but it was the right thing to do.

"We provide services for this kind of situation," the doctor explained. "Whatever you need."

I leaned down and gave Cairo a warm rub on the back.

"Thank you," I said. "But we'll take care of it. I want to take him home."

I scooped Cairo up, carried him outside, and loaded him into the truck. Natalie and I drove him home, the miles unfurling in silence. I carried him into the house and gently placed him on his bed. I gave him an injection of a painkiller to help him feel more comfortable. Then I made a phone call to one of the navy vet technicians and asked him for a favor. A short time later he arrived and began laying out the tools and medication he would need to euthanize Cairo. Natalie and I both lay down on the floor next to him and stroked his head. I took his paw in my hand.

"Everything is going to be okay, buddy."

It was over quickly and painlessly. On April 2, 2015, at 3:20 in the afternoon, Cairo slipped peacefully away, surrounded by his family, with Daddy holding his hand.

"I love you," I said through tears. It didn't matter that he couldn't hear me. My head was pressed against his. He could feel me. He knew I was there.

Afterward, the vet tech told us about a woman who lived not far away. She ran a small crematorium business out of her rural home. Her clients were mostly people like us, who had lost beloved family pets. She would help us with Cairo's remains. As Natalie and I drove up to her house, with Cairo in the back seat, wrapped in his favorite blanket, a sweet, sad song poured out of the radio. It was Adele's cover of "Make You Feel My Love," written by Bob Dylan.

"I'd go hungry, I'd go black and blue
To make you feel my love."

The woman who owned the business welcomed us into her home. She said she was very sorry, and then asked to see Cairo. She promised to take good care of him.

A couple of days later, we returned to her house to pick up Cairo's remains. In a large coffee can, with paw prints and his name written on the side, were Cairo's ashes. Another can contained a handful of screws and a metal plate. This was the hardware that had been implanted during surgery after Cairo was wounded in Afghanistan. The metal hadn't disintegrated in the crematorium. It was a reminder of Cairo's bravery.

There was also a plaster impression of his paw print, and a small, tight bundle of Cairo's hair intended for Natalie.

"This is for you," the woman said with a smile as she pushed it across the counter.

We gathered everything together in a box and thanked her for her kindness. She knew that I was a navy guy, but I don't think she knew I was a SEAL, or that Cairo was a working dog. She certainly didn't know of his many accomplishments. If she had asked, I would have told her:

Cairo lived a great life.

He was a heroic working dog and a faithful companion.

I can honestly say I could not have asked for a better dog. Or a better friend. He never knew what he had accomplished or the lives he saved, but he knew that he made people happy.

And that was the most important thing to him.

EPILOGUE

You can't rush recovery.

Whether you're talking about the head or the heart, healing takes time. Grief goes out like the tide, leaving memories that make you smile or laugh. Life is for the living, after all, and you can only walk around in a daze for so long.

On July 31, 2015, nearly four months after Cairo passed away, my medical retirement finally came through. After so many months of waiting, it was strangely anticlimactic.

It felt like a long time since I'd been a Navy SEAL. I say that with no anger or regret. The simple truth is, I enlisted in the navy as a boy fresh out of high school and chased the dream of becoming a SEAL with everything I had. I did it because I wanted to serve my country at the highest possible level.

Was that naive or simplistic? Maybe a little. The world is a lot more complicated than I realized when I left Texas. I didn't know what it was like to kill someone or to watch my friends die. But I believe in the work that we did, and I remain proud of my contributions. I am grateful for the opportunity to have served alongside men I can honestly say are the best of the best.

But three years had passed since I held the job I signed up for; there was no way I would ever again be healthy or young enough to go back to it. It's strange to feel like an old man at thirty-one years of age, but that's the way it was for me.

And the navy agreed.

My career came to an end quietly and gradually, with three years of limited service. None of it involved jumping out of planes or chasing bad guys or blowing things up. I was wounded. I suffered a traumatic brain injury. It happens.

I tried not to feel sorry for myself. It could have been a whole lot worse. More than ninety members of the Naval Special Warfare community have been killed in action or during training exercises since 9/11. Hundreds more have been seriously wounded. They struggle today with scars far more damaging than mine.

In so many ways, I was lucky. I tried to remind myself of that fact—even on the very worst days.

After my retirement was official, I took a security job in Alabama. That was a mistake. It was much too soon. The headaches worsened, and the brain fog rolled in. After six months, I left the job and filled the next year traveling with Natalie and the dogs. We spent time with her family in Florida and my family in Texas. We visited friends in various places around the country. Eventually we bought a little house on a lake in East Texas.

Through friends in the navy, I found a place in Dallas called the Brain Treatment Foundation. This is an organization that provides support to combat veterans suffering from traumatic brain injuries and post-traumatic stress. A lot of vets struggle with symptoms related to their service. They often feel like they have to suffer in silence. Alone. I felt that way a lot of the time. But there is help, and I was fortunate to find it. I'd like to help others find it, as well.

I also received help from the Brain Treatment Center in

California. I tried a lot of different therapy. Over time, I began to heal. The headaches and back spasms receded. Freed from chronic pain, I weaned myself off most medication. My mood naturally lifted.

I still get headaches sometimes. There are days when I think about the friends I have lost, and the cloud rolls in. But it passes. I don't stay in the dark for long. My memory is better than it has been in years. I feel . . . better. Almost whole again.

Natalie and I added two more dogs to the family: another Malinois and a Dutch shepherd. They're cute, and they keep us busy. Sometimes one of the Malinois will cross one paw over the other and tilt its head a certain way and the resemblance to Cairo is uncanny.

And it makes me smile.

Occasionally, I have to travel for work. I take freelance security assignments, and I'm working with the Brain Treatment Foundation to encourage veterans to seek help. Sometimes I'll take one of the dogs on the road with me. But even when they stay at home, I am rarely alone.

That coffee can with the paw print? The one that contains Cairo's ashes? I usually carry it in my backpack when I'm on the road. I drive almost everywhere. Doesn't matter if the trip is two hundred miles or two thousand miles. I'd rather sit behind the wheel and roll down the windows and crank the music. Once in a while, though, I am forced to fly. It hasn't happened often, but there have been a couple of times when I have taken Cairo with me, which has caused some interesting reactions at airport security.

> TSA Screener (holding up coffee can, looking at paw prints): "What's this?"
>
> Me: "That's my dog, sir. He was my best friend."
>
> TSA Screener (gently placing can back on table): "Oh . . . I'm sorry."
>
> Me: "That's okay. He goes everywhere with me."
>
> TSA Screener (nodding sympathetically): "I understand."

He doesn't really understand, of course. But then, how could he? I never tell anyone that the can contains the ashes of not just any dog but one of the most amazing dogs who ever lived. That's something I've always sort of kept to myself.

Lately, though, I've thought that it would be nice if more people knew about Cairo and had a chance to hear his story. Maybe they could connect with him in some way. I've been thinking about donating some of my personal memorabilia to the 9/11 Memorial, including reminders of my time with Cairo. I still have the blood-stained harness he wore the night he saved my life, and that he later wore during Operation Neptune Spear. It would be hard to part with that, but it would be a fitting tribute to Cairo if others had a chance to see it.

Maybe I'll donate his ashes, as well, or at least a portion of his ashes. I'd like to keep some for myself, tucked safely in a coffee can in my backpack, so that Cairo is never far away, and so that he will always know . . .

I love you, buddy.

ACKNOWLEDGMENTS

I want to thank everyone who came together to make this book possible. It has been a pleasure working with my editor, Marc Resnick; his assistant, Hannah O'Grady; and the entire team at St. Martin's Press who worked so hard to put this project together. Also thanks to Jean Feiwel and Kat Brzozowski at Feiwel & Friends. It's been a long road!

My cowriter, Joe Layden, has made the difficult process of telling Cairo's story much easier and even enjoyable at times. As much as I miss Cairo, it has been rewarding to have an opportunity to share memories of our time together.

Special thanks to producers Mark Semos and Jay Pollak from the Reserve Label and Cairo Holdings, and a big thank-you to producer Alan Rautbort. And thanks also to our literary agent, Frank Weimann.

I would like to thank the US Navy and the SEAL teams for allowing me to serve my country and giving me the opportunity to participate in countless great events. I want to thank my teammates for always being there, and their families for allowing them to be. I would like to acknowledge everyone who served or who is currently serving in any capacity, keeping this country safe. Most notably, I want to recognize my fallen brothers in the military who have made the ultimate sacrifice.

I would also like to thank everyone who has helped me get through the difficult times transitioning out of the navy, both on a personal and medical side. Natalie Kelley was there for me (and Cairo) when I needed a lot of support, and I will always be grateful. There were many doctors and support personnel at various treatment centers I attended; your kindness and expertise meant the world to me and helped me on the path to recovery. Among this group I would like to specifically recognize Kara Williams and the staff of the Brain Treatment Foundation for all their hard work on behalf of veterans. There are many other friends and teammates who helped on a personal level; too many to name individually here, and I don't want to leave anyone out. You know who you are!

I would like to thank my mother and father for providing me with a loving home and family, and for supporting my decision to enter the navy and chase my dream of becoming a SEAL. Thanks for always being there for me.

Finally, I would like to thank God for watching over me through times good and bad.

Thank you for reading this Feiwel and Friends book. The Friends who made *Warrior Dog* possible are:

Jean Feiwel, Publisher

Liz Szabla, Associate Publisher

Rich Deas, Senior Creative Director

Mallory Grigg, Art Director

Holly West, Senior Editor

Anna Roberto, Senior Editor

Kat Brzozowski, Senior Editor

Alexei Esikoff, Senior Managing Editor

Kim Waymer, Senior Production Manager

Erin Siu, Assistant Editor

Emily Settle, Associate Editor

Rachel Diebel, Assistant Editor

Foyinsi Adegbonmire, Editorial Assistant

Follow us on Facebook or visit us online at mackids.com.

Our books are friends for life